PEN

A Provocative Poetic Journey

Trishforreal

Pen: *A Provocative Poetic Journey* is written by Trishforreal.
All rights reserved. Published 2021.
ISBN: 978-0-578-97677-8
LIBRARY OF CONGRESS CONTROL NUMBER: 2021917337
COPYRYIGHT© TRISHFORREAL

COVER IMAGE USED UNDER LICENSE BY SHUTTERSTOCK.COM

No part of this publication may be replicated or transmitted in any form or by any means, electronic or mechanical, including photocopy, recording, or any information storage and retrieval system, without the publisher's written permission.

DEDICATION

To Rouchelle Deux, thank you for your constancy and unconditional love. You have constantly reminded me to pour out this gift implanted within me by God. Thank you for being a loyal friend in all seasons of my life.

To Vennessa, thank you for your selflessness and for being my light and voice of reason in my low places. Tuffy and Jimmy made you for me.

To the many people who will get entranced on this poetic journey through my thoughts and emotions, I hope you have a fantastic encounter.

About Pen

You are invited on a provocative, poetic journey through the thoughts and emotions of the poet. *Pen* is divided into four moving parts:

- Part One: Love and the in-betweens
- Part Two: Nostalgia
- Part Three: Proverbs for Life
- Part Four: The Mind of the Poet

Each part is nuanced and has its own vehicle through imagination. May your senses be awakened as you travel through this multi-layered world of self-expression, expansion, and humanity.

Pen Is...

- RAW
- SINUOUS
- PROVERBIAL
- PHILOSOPHICAL
- IMAGINATIVE
- NOSTALGIC
- MOVING
- MULTI-LAYERED
- PROVOCATIVE

From the Poet

As I look back over my life, one thing remains true: I always have a pen with me. It almost comes second nature. Talk about feeling bare without it! No matter the emotion I experience, I will write about it in my journal. As I began to search for a title for this project, I stumbled upon an image of a clenched fist with a pen. I was sold at first sight. I wanted a title that would evoke power and provoke thought.

I once heard that the pen is the greatest weapon because it has the power to change worlds. I couldn't agree more. The pen has changed my world since the time I was nine years old. Rightly so, the pen is my weapon of choice. When all else fails, words rarely fail me. I named this book *Pen* because of my deep love for writing poetry. The pen bids self-expression to escape from every chasm of my spirit; it brings every follicle of my imagination to life. I am at my happiest, most vulnerable, and authentic self when I hold my pen.

From the time I was a little girl, I have heard that my words are my gift. As I became more aware of my purpose, I sought to embrace and expand this gift. I still remember my pen pals days. Before social media, video chat, emails, and instant messages became the way of life, the pen was the instrument of communication. To this day, I still have a trinket box filled with every handwritten letter sent to me. I write to connect my audience to my most fragile thoughts and the fragments of my past and present realities. *Pen* bleeds my angst and hope for the future and my call to action. I believe the poet's work is to provoke thought. I write to honor the gift entrusted to me by God. I hope *Pen* stirs your empathy and imagination.

I wish you the courage to use your gifts to change the world through honor and compassion for all men.

From my spirit,

TRISHFORREAL

Hello poetry enthusiast! Welcome to a provocative, poetic journey. Enter a world of self-expression and imagination.

Part One

LOVE AND THE IN-BETWEENS

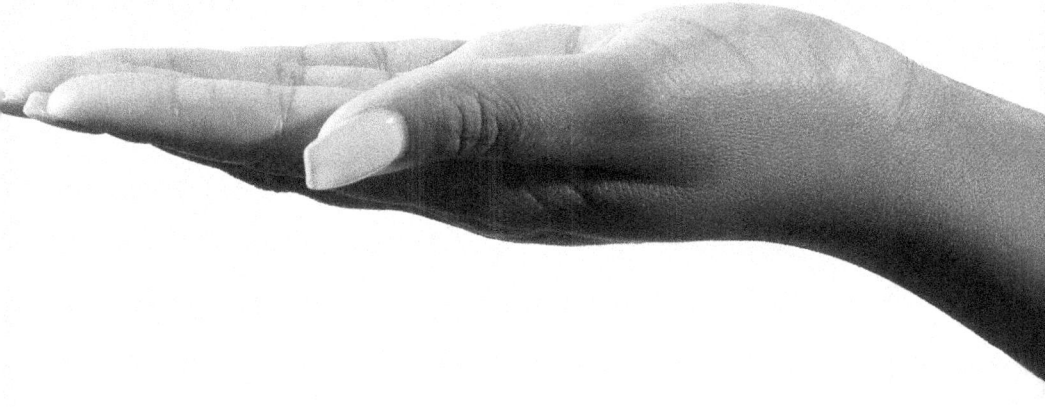

Entryway to Paradise

Should I marvel at your promise of paradise,
When my heart is set aflame
With your intentions of grandeur,
Girded by a solemn vow to tame and conquer the monster within me?
Is there such a thing as halfway to heaven,
Or do I sit at the entryway
Until you decide to let me into paradise?

Tell me, dear lover,
When you sit on the throne of my heart,
Would you hold out your scepter to the fool
Left with an empty pledge of happiness?
Who did you take to paradise,
Your espoused or another of your many lovers?
Is your heart left in paradise,
Or is it like mine posted in front of passion's door?
Whom do you enchant
When it isn't me, you lure
Into your frivolous trap?

No man arouses a wasp nest without getting stung.
When we were on the banks of the Euphrates,
Did the water not kiss your face as it did mine?
Did you not walk amidst
The cedars of Lebanon with me?
Tell me, lover, did we not
Taste the nectar of heaven on earth?

And if we indeed did get raptured in bliss,
Would you not want to feel the feel again,
Or do you want to leave at the entryway to paradise?

Anchored Love

Show me the scars engraved upon your heart.
Take me to the depths of your soul
Where your gravest secret lies,
The place light hasn't been.
Give me a glimpse of what's inside—
Inside your Pandora box.
But no matter what I find in the midst,
I won't run,
I won't hide.
Instead, I will give you an anchor to dock.
But tell me, my love,
If you were to come to harbor,
Close to the edge of paradise,
The place where I lay my head,
Will you burden my pillow with worry?
And if love were foreign to you
And your baggage were burdensome,
Would you throw it overboard
And unmask the frailty of your soul to me?

Bosomed Lover

Lover on whose bosom I shall rest,
I will journey home tonight.
Bathe yourself in spices—
Choose lavender or maybe myrrh.
Oh, I will be nesting on your bosom tonight!
Lonely was I in a faraway land,
Crippled by longing
And bursting at the seams with lust and need.
Still, I waited as though in travail,
Not knowing when I will break the water of passion.

Take me to the starlight tonight,
Cause I have dreamed of your magic
And to be engulfed in your charm.
Lullaby me in your slumber,
And adorn your body with ornaments and oils.
Open your private closet to me, sweet dove.
Be the salve for my wounded soul,
The milk and honey for my hungry belly.
I seek to pick your lilies and unveil your treasures.
But if you are restrained by virtue,
I will return to unmask my desire,
To lay upon your bosom
And to be held captive by your kiss of caramel
And honey clusters.
Then you may give me your breast as a pillow
And your love as my bed.

"Lullaby me in your slumber and adorn your body with ornaments and oils."

The One

Rest your hands on my thighs,
While I bury my back against your chest.
Feel my neck nestled on your collarbone,
As our breaths get in sync.
I am in heaven—
Because time stops when I am with you.
You are sunrise,
Shade in the heat,
The warmth of summer,
Health, to my soul.
I asked the sage how I would know
You were sent for me,
And he asked me if our hearts beat as one
When we touch.
I said, "Yes. My lover breathes magic."
"Then, he is the one," said the oracle.

Tainted Rose

Enchanted by your beauty, I was
And lured by your charm.
Somehow, I have failed to see
Your one remaining thorn.
Tainted, you still are by your prickle.
Oh, sweet-smelling rose,
Your fragrance lingers
As well as the piercing of your thorn.

Could you not warn me that
Beautiful things are sometimes tainted too;
That the eye that beholds the beauty
Can neglect the piercing of its thorn?
Could you, by your own doing,
Have escaped the pruning shear?
Can you not see it? Do you not know it-
That you, oh rose of my garden,
Is marred by a single thorn, a sharp spine?

Pauper

I loved a lover who didn't like me,
Used a band-aid to cover a rude, festering sore,
Cursed my mother and treated a virgin
As though she were a courtesan.
I carried a bag up a hill, you see,
Only to tumble down the mountain again.

I hated a friend who loved me
While I gave my treasures to a foe.
What is a joke to you is death to me.
Hate made my stomach sore,
And love was like vinegar to my thirst.
My heart was like a cistern holding bitter and sweet.

I gave a loan I didn't have to deepen a hole
That was already in my pocket.
It made my cupboard empty,
Empty and bare,
But I never complained, never complained.
My heart pauperized me and buried me in guilt
Because I was made naked
By a promise I couldn't keep.

Maiden

Midnight came quite early,
And I lost my borrowed slippers
Way before I laid eyes on not Prince Charming,
But a frog longing for a kiss.
I was too jaded from the weight of my mind
And the yearning for passion.
I was trapped within the walls of discontent,
Barricaded by time fleeced.
The smell of herbs and spices, the traces of oil,
The residue of ashes lingered on my hands.
My face, a reservoir of anguish and bitter longing.
A sense of wilful duty imprisoned me,
I dreaded each moment, each escaping thought.

My heart had waxed cold between two bonfires of regret.
Then, a sudden shift in the wind brought with it
A lightness that was almost foreign.
We became two strangers
Who once breathed the same air.
As light flooded each dark crevice of my heart,
Glee quickly budded, and peace returned.
My lover awoke from his godforsaken slumber
To find a swept house, unwrinkled sheets
And pots of glory.

He smiled as if pleased and timidly asked me
To go to the river.
We, slowly, walked to the river
And we both submerged to heal our leprous union.
We went under as enemies and came out as friends.

My Favorite Place

If I could hang one picture on the walls of time,
It would be the way you smile when I look at you.
If I could write one song for you,
I would title it "I Choose You."
You and I love like a song
With our favorite lyrics, beat, and tune.
You and I love like a poem
Which catapults us into a world only you and I know.
If I could write you the perfect phrase,
It would say,
You are the answer to my prayer.

I carry you on my heart
Like a mother carrying her young.
I kiss you while you are sleeping,
Sprinkle peace over your head,
And ask God to allow you
To complete your life's work.
I keep you safe like a secret made known only to God.
In the moments when hope is lost,
I will use my light to guide your path.
You are the perfect melody,
The greatest song, my favorite place, my one true love.

And if your tomorrow comes before mine,
I promise to share our story with the world.
They would know that love is beautiful,
But not for the faint of heart.
I love you, my love,
With even the faintest whisper of my soul.

Canvas

Come, let me paint you with words from my soul
And hand you gems from my heart's overflow.

Come, let me draw you a picture of your dreams
And hang them on a scaffold with beams
Of hope, love, laughter, and sunny skies.

Come, let me chase away the blues and your cries
With love sonnets and lofty words.

Come, let me give you courage as color on a canvas
To add joy to your heart and lighten up your soul.

If you should return to your folly,
Glance upon the portrait and dream again.
Follow where the rainbow leads.
Hang flowers somewhere or reeds
To bring you back to love and this masterpiece,
A canvas drenched with words written only for you.

Mr. Burt

If I go back in moments,
Memories seem to stop
At the instant, you came into my life.
I relive that minute quite often.
You are the reason I love, my answered prayer.

Though words haven't been spoken,
You reveal so much in your deeds,
In your excitement, your gaze.
Even after a reproof, you are ever close,
Teaching me more about love
Than I ever did know.

In happy moments, you are there.
In sad times, you pull closer,
As if to assure me that we are in it together.

One thing remains true:
I have never met a friend like you.

Big Daddy

I want to call you Big Daddy,
Serve you breakfast on me,
And then ask you to do me nasty.
I want to meet you by the door in heels,
Wearing a trench coat
And nothing else.

Let's spread out some silk sheets,
Double skeet, skeet,
Jump on it back and forth.
I want to give you the red light special
And talk dirty for hours,
Cause the kids are away, and it's just us—

Us and these four or eight walls,
The kitchen, the bathroom, down the hall,
A dozen red roses and a steamy hot bath.
I want to play some 80s or 90s love songs
And relive our first kiss,
And the moment when you popped the cherry,
Ate the mango,
And I said," Oh bliss!"

I want to sing "Freak Like Me,"
Then whisper sweet everythings in your ear
Until I hear you say,
"Quit playing, and let me show you who's your Daddy."
Oh Daddy, behave!

Rhapsody

Let's stargaze as my spirit is raptured,
Raptured by the strum of your guitar,
The smell of Kush on your lips and skin.
Come closer, so I can taste your breath,
Lock my eyes with yours
As our hearts get in tune.

I feel the rhythm of your heart.
It beats like a drum—
As you pull me into rhapsody.
Oh, honey, your soul is beautiful.
It smells like peppermint and lavender.

I saw the color of your thoughts.
They look like surrender,
Surrender to the ebb and the flow of this love.
Your thoughts smell like the crisp ocean breeze,
Sage, citrus, honeysuckle, and coconut.
You are serendipity.
Oh, you feel like home to me.

"You are serendipity. Oh, you feel like home to me."

Red Roses

I bought a dozen red roses for my damn self.
That's self-care for me.
Wait on who, you, for what— Love?
No chile.

I bought a dozen red roses for my damn self.
That's therapy for me.
You see, my man went out and bought cigarettes,
So I went out and got myself red wine and red roses.
"What's the occasion?" he asked.
I answered, "Me time."

I bought a dozen red roses for my damn self.
I'm over here radiating this bliss of heaven,
But he's over there looking at me like I'm crazy.
"Who bought you those?" he asked.
"Me, myself, and I," I said.
The fool didn't notice when I needed them
But cared how I got them.

I bought a dozen red roses for my damn self
Because I dressed up to feel some type of way about myself.
The joker hasn't touched me in weeks,
And there's a gulf in the middle of our bed.
He said, "Where have you been? What we goin' eat?"
 "I'm not hungry," I said.
He asked, "How was the date?"
I went to the room.

I bought a dozen white roses for my damn self.
Ain't no use waking the dead,

So I cooked my favorite food and set the table for one, one.
As soon as he came through the door,
He said, "Is this what you cooked? I don't eat that."
I said, "I know.
It's for me, sugah!"
He went to the bathroom and took a long shower.

The following week, the stranger came home with twelve dozen red roses, a bottle of vintage red wine,
And takeout and paid for my weave.
I let him in close enough until I heard him say,
"Who is the nigga you've been seeing?" "I said, "Me."

Et Tu, Brute

Even you, a friend of my heart?
Even you, whose tears like a river
Once filled my collarbone?
Even you, a friend of my bosom, whom I fed manna
No one else has seen the likes of?
Even you, you, you, you!

You drank from my cup and laid on my bosom
During the winters of your many distresses.
We walked crooked paths together,
Journeyed on together,
Even when no manna fell from the sky.
We walked into the council of friendship.
I gave you my only coat.
I wept for you when your enemies tried to overtake you.

I loved you like myself,
And would have given you a rib if you asked.
When you were happy
And when your success came,
I danced and burst out into song
As though it were mine.

But when I became king of my destiny,
You poured me spikenard,
You conspired to have me killed.
I smelled the guile on your lips
When you came to kiss me.
The trails of the venom on your tongue
Pierced my heart like a dagger.

Was it the gift in me
That stirred up so much anger in you, my friend?
Tell me, dearest Judas,
Was it my chance at success and happiness
That sent you on a devil's rampage?
Did you think you could take something from me
That you didn't give in the first place?
You handed me a yellow rose
While you impaled me with a thousand knives.
One stab in the back from a friend
Is like giving a thirsty dog an empty bowl.

Et Tu, Brute?
Friend, is that you or is it Judas Iscariot?
For what have you come?
Did you not get your thirty pieces
When you sold me
To the herd of evil men who plotted my demise?
Even you, my friend?
They bought you too, Brutus?
Was it worth the profit you gained
When you took me to the devil's auction
To pass me off to jackals and thieves?

Even in my anger,
I asked God to withhold the vengeance
You do deserve.
You see, I am still in the whirling wind you left me in.
You too, my friend?
I pray maggots and worms may feast on your carcass
That even vultures may turn from the stench of the guilt that surrounds even your rotten corpse,
Et Tu, Brute?
Even you, my friend?

Cupid

I gave Cupid my last dollar
For a chance at love;
And borrowed Cinderella's only slipper
For eternal happiness,
To behold a spark that didn't last.
A lion fleeced me out as prey.
Cupid was his name.
He turned out to be a farce
Whose mouth is a snare.
He quickly vanished in the dead of night
With both his promise and my virtue.
Cupid turned out to be an empty oath.

Achilles Heel

I disrobed before my lover to show him my scarlet letter
Lodged between my thighs.
I opened the darkest places of my heart to him.
I gave him a glimpse of my soul,
And let him hold my breath for a second,
But all that was dung to him,
Something for the piles of trash
Taken by him as relics.

My lover was a headless demon,
A walking dead roaming in earnest
With the intent to take off my head
And leave a pike in my heart.
You vile Praying Mantis!
Couldn't you have warned me that chivalry was an ensnarement?

Now, I traverse like a headless fool whose soul was sucked out by a vermin.
I will wait for him at dark and take back my heart
And head from his treasure chest;
Then I will cut his Achilles heel.

Now I know why the scribe had said,
"Do not have tea with the devil.
He will come back for payment on a day you least expect."
That day had come,
And the monster came through a crack
And brought with it a tsunami
That destroyed every pillar and post of my refuge.
Never forget that an idle mind is the devil's nest.
Do not bring your pearls to visit a hog.

Catcher's Lure

Sorrow was the pillow that held my head
After my lover betrayed me;
It was the bottle for my tears
And the meal I ate many a night.
You see, my love, now an enemy
Became a thorn in my flesh, my silent grief.
Sorrow was my most trustworthy companion
During the winter of my soul.
It was a drought brought on
By one espoused to me,
One on whom I bestowed all
My affection and avowed
The most profound depth of my soul.
Sorrow was the country
I journeyed to, to be with my enchanter,
And to drink from the winery of paradise
And eat of its honeycombs;
But when I destined there, my eyes were shocked by
A famine and barrenness,
Of a hope not resurrected.
Sorrow had become the bed
Of the lover who jilted me
For the lure of a catcher's bait,
Only to be left with a flickering
Of an image never again to be beheld.

Love

Love is a smooth path,
A winding road,
A deep valley,
A sinking ship.

Love is a bickering woman,
A quiet lady,
A laboring hand,
A gleaming stare.

Love is a crooked path,
A blinding view,
A secret cavern,
A never-ending cliff.

Love is a pillaging thief,
A lonely path,
A faithful dog,
A cloak in winter.

Love is a narrow bridge,
A tightening cocoon,
The whisper of a bird,
A lover's kiss.

She Walked Away

She didn't forget her past; she had only tucked it away. She knew she couldn't take back the pieces of her heart she had so recklessly given away, so she wore what was left on her sleeve as a reminder to never again prostitute her power. The wounds inflicted in the game of love were still fresh. She alone could see the arrow still lodged between her heart and her will to move on.

Again, she walked away from everything and everyone that wouldn't add value in the new season of her life. She envisioned beautiful tomorrows, but she knew it would be days before shedding the things which once were but were no more. She's become a walking reservoir of lost hope but greater possibilities. With regrets all packed and the invisible sword in her hand, she is traveling light. She is woman, survivor, and Queen!

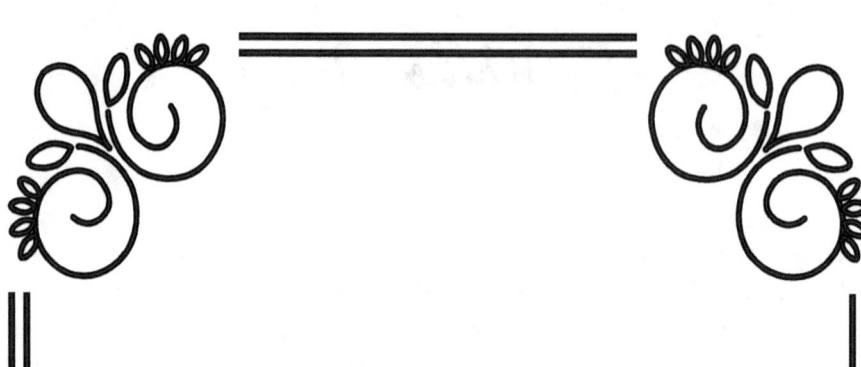

"She is woman, survivor, and Queen!"

Dirty Sport

She wanted a Cinderella love story.
The type where she would wake up from a daydream,
Receive help from her guides,
Morph into something beautiful,
And find a picture-perfect love—
But she lost it in the nick of time,
Languished over a temporary loss
Then went back into the shadows alone.

Nobody told her love's a murky sport,
Not for the faint of heart,
Not for the one who is afraid to lose it or risk it all.
It brings you high and takes you down low.
It rages war and sometimes has you at the mercy of surrender.
Kings have lost their kingdoms over a drink of love;
Healthy men have lost their vigor over the beguiling of women.
Love is a muddy sport,
The hurter sometimes has the balm,
And the frog could be the prince.

Love on Life Support

Just like that, their love coded.
The alarms went off,
And the discovery was made
That their love was only built on quicksand.
The storms came to show
That their love wasn't strong enough
To endure what was ahead.

Their love was on life support.
He did; she did, and they both did things they wished they could undo.
Lies were spoken,
Hearts got broken, boundaries were crossed,
And then the bags were packed
With the baggage they had both begun with,
And what they amassed from being together.

In the beginning, it was a thrill.
They had found a love that made them
Sail among the stars and at times touch heaven.
Love was their escape from a past unconquered,
One deeply rooted in pain and disappointment.
Theirs was like a love song set on repeat,
Lullabies, hearts that pant at the rush of new love.

It was paradise, Caribbean breeze,
Hot cocoa on a cold night.
Now its stale beer, a lingering cough, bickering, disputing,
Two bedrooms in one, hard stares, hearts bursting with bitterness and regrets,
an empty dinner table, an aperture in the middle of the bed.
The house has become a den of torment, loud silence, and short sleep.
One lover walked away;
The other remained frozen.

I Wish

I wish I could kiss away the cold from your cheeks,
Hold your hands
And listen to the speed of your heartbeat.
I wish I could sing you a song
Or two to make merry your heart
And chase the dark clouds away.
I wish I could bring you a needed sigh of relief
On days too uncertain to gamble on,
And on nights when mornings seem too far in the distance.
I wish I could hear the whisper of a secret
Known only to me,
One of deep sorrow and shame.
I feel pain as telling as the loss of a lover
Who never returned from war,
Whose shoes by the bed have gone old,
Rotten down to its very sole.
I wish I could tell you of the longing
I have had to hold your gaze,
As you look deep into my eyes with questions and knowing.

And if we ever do meet again,
I wish I could freeze the moment for eternity.
And if I open my eyes to see
It's but a dream,
I pray you to tell God to rock you in his arms for me.

Distant Lover

Winter felt long last year,
But what felt longer were the cold nights
I spent alone with
A lover who had grown distant right beside me.
My lover has succumbed to
The harlot's sting,
Had eaten the poisonous apple
And like Snow White had fallen asleep
Under the curse of passion.
His body was buried beside me,
But his mind and spirit
Were sheltered in the bosom
Of the one whom he loved.
I kept waking him up
But no pulse could be felt.
I pulled over my covers
And laid there with the dead.

Kind of Love

I want an ah kind of love,
A toe-curling, knee-shaking type of love,
A souls' meeting kind of love,
A heart-racing with each gaze at you, kind of love,
Drooling over you, I can't get enough of you, kind of love.

I want a Danielle Steel, a lifetime movie kind of love,
A Harlequin romance kind of love.
I want a fool's rush in kind of love,
That lovers leap type of love,
That paging you 1-2-3 kind of love.

I want a nothing separates us, kind of love,
That me for you and you for me kind of love.
I want a move mountains for, your kind of love,
That we are working this thing out kind of love,
That if it isn't you, there's no us kind of love.

I want that pick up on one ring kind of love—
That I want to fall asleep on the phone kind of love.
They can have that social media buzz kind of love,
Cause baby, what we have is you put a move on me kind of love.

I want a no sharing your kind of love,
That tell me whose is it kind of love,
That have you on speed dial kind of love,
That Romeo and Juliet kind of love,
That Shakespeare Sonnet XVI kind of love,
That ooh la la kind of love.

I want that oh sh** kind of love,
That, oh Jesus, kind of love,
That deep fall kind of love,
That if you don't have it, I got it kind of love.
Give me that party for two kind love,
That no outsider can penetrate this kind of love.
You know that love?
That love! That love!

Our Love

I have loved you, love, in, through, and out.
I have loved you, love,
In the sun and the rain.
Oh, I have loved you, love,
When the nightingales sang us sweet lullabies,
And when the winds brought us hope.

I have loved you, love,
In the hardest of times,
In safe harbor and high tide.
It was us, us against the mountains, love.
You and me.
You and me.

I have loved you in spring, summer,
Autumn, and in winter's blues.
I have loved you, love, with holes in your pockets and your shoes.

I have loved you, love,
When we had to feel our way through the dark
And swim in muddied waters.
Oh, I have loved you, love in the up and the down,
Around and beneath,
And when you were not so lovely, love.

I have loved you, love,
As we mixed the bitter with the sweet,
Come wind, sun, or sleet.

Oh, I have loved you love with and without,
In want and plenty,
To the moon and back,
In the still and the storm.
I have loved you love for your quiet ease and your cool melody.
I have loved you, love through and through, then, and now.
Oh, I— will love you, love, forever and a year.

Kiss of Death

I thought I heard the kiss of death on a day
While I lay in the forest, contemplating my lover's goodbye.
I thought I felt when it touched
My hand and whispered, "Let's go to the light."
Was it death who knocked at my heart's door,
When I was drunk from despair;
Or was it my own mind
Which pushed me to the brink of madness?
My lover had jilted me for my neighbor,
One whom I had fed choice meats
And secrets from my heart and of him.
My lover had brought on the crucible of my life.
Death returned to kiss me,
But I turned away my cheeks.

Oasis

Bury yourself in the cleft of my oasis,
Within the cocoon of my desire.
Glide your fingers along the borders that will take you to my promised land.
Drink the milk of my passion
And eat of its honey.
Speak to me slowly and let me hear
What lies beyond utterance,
What dwells in the deep seas of your heart.
Breathe, my love, then kiss me.

Hold me as though I were awakened from an eternal sleep,
Or returning from a prodigious pilgrimage.
Kiss me, my love.
Let me breathe your breath and take your thoughts as tea; choice tea:
Traded over open waters and adorned by the kiss of the sun.
Let's take a walk in the garden of love,
Where the moon will adorn my skin with the hue of heaven,
And where the stars will show you my Milky Way.

Rapture me, my love!
Let's go in search of Aladdin and borrow his carpet.
Let's see the world from the skies, touch the moon, caress the stars and then return to the refuge of our love.
Let's stay here forever.

Hieros Gamos

She wanted to be found in places where she was most ruined, most fragile, and most deprived. Still, she waited with the kind of knowing that those who came to ensnare her were not the one she had prayed for, the sacred love.

Then she met him unexpectedly. His thorns curtsied at her touch. They somehow knew that she came to love. She was his goddess, and they were experiencing the Hieros gamos, the most sacred of all loves. He let her into places no one had gone before, and she held onto his love like a flower and spread out her canopy over its fragility. She, too, had pain and anguish hidden too far for him to see. He also had let her into his secret places, places where love was an intruder. They both had for too long accepted love's antithesis; now, they had given each other all the love they had. They were awakened to a deeper kind of love that could not be physically expressed. It was a passion unchartered before now.

They often questioned whether this newness was for them. How could two people so similar in nature have found each other? Somehow, the gods had favored them this time. No lover before mattered. They had each gone through the crucible of pain and regret to get to a love that defies their understanding. Theirs was a love that was freeing, pure, not wanting anything but to love. And each night, as they held each other in a sweet embrace, they cried tears of joy.

In her silent whisper, God heard her say, "It was good that I was afflicted by love, so that I may partake in your gift of scared love. I am forever grateful that you found it fit to bless me." As soon as her prayers ended, he bathed her in kisses and anointed her head with oil. He, too, had prayed that he would be the greatest love she'd ever known and extolled God for gifting him with his desired love.

"HIS THORNS CURTSIED AT HER TOUCH. THEY SOMEHOW KNEW THAT SHE CAME TO LOVE."

Desire

Let me breathe you,
Taste the nectar of your soul,
Lick the licorice cascading
Down the sides of your mouth.
Oh, you are a fortress of budding desire;
You are my deep yearning,
My favorite song, my refuge.
Let's make passion burst;
Let's fill our cups with love—
How does my honey taste?
What of my milk that has you eager to feed?
Do you see the sunshine between my legs
And the baring of my soul?

Put your head on my pillow, silly dove.
Let the softness put you to slumber.
Our passion's like the candle by our bed—
Snuffed out by the wind of our breaths.
Let's cradle my love;
Hold me as tightly as your darkest secret.
Whisper your desire in my ear,
So I can go to the edge of pleasure
And explode with the waters of our love.
Feel me again, my love.
Pluck the rose from my thorns.
Come to roost, stay in my cocoon.
The night is still young
And outside is cold.

EveryWoman's Story

"Baby, I need you to change," were the last words she said to him, the man she had married and chose above all others. Yes, plenty of others were better suited, but she bit the apple of his charm and fell for his sweet lies. After her last cry for change, she buried herself into an open tomb. You see, everyone who passed by could see and smell what was hidden beyond make-belief. Happiness was foreign to her. She wasn't happy with this and with that. Before long, she ran out of faith and buried herself with the dead thing, a union that had long passed on.

She was faithful to him, but that loyalty was like powdering a black bird. She wasted years trying to wake up the dead. Still, he only offered her contrived efforts, a few fake apologies, and empty promises. And even though the marriage bed was paralyzed, she was still trying to do breaststrokes in the desert. She loved this two-timing joker to the point of ruin. She would have given him a rib if he'd asked.

He, like sleeping beauty, had eaten the witch's poison and had fallen dead asleep on his wife but was somehow alive to his other women. No amount of sexy lingerie could awaken the dead. No Brazilian waxing, nude pics, sexting, sexual gestures, or innuendos could get a pulse from Lazarus. Lazarus was gone, and the tomb he slept in began to stink. She said Psalms for him, thinking this time Jesus would himself weep for Lazarus, but the only tear flowing was her very own. She prayed for his return, wrote many Dear God letters, but God remained silent.

She, too, became a carcass trying to get the old thing back. Rigor mortis had already set in, and everyone around noticed what was already putrefying with them. She trained herself to be numb and to take moments of a reprieve even amid a crowd. He had inflicted blow after blow to her soul until the light within her went dim. The very fragrance of her soul smelled like decay and bitter regret, but she didn't notice. She remained frozen and said no more words to him.

She became silent because she was done nursing the dead. Silence turned into bitterness, and bitterness turned into fury. She became angry at herself for giving what was sacred to a dog. Within this moment of truth, she awakened from her godforsaken slumber and said, "Let's burn this shit to ashes." She knew that only God could beautify her ashes, so she left them at his feet. The sleeping dog jumped up from his sleep and said, 'Release me," to which she quickly replied, "I freely release you. Adieu!"

The ties that held them together were finally severed, and her light returned. She was whole again.

Part Two

Proverbs for Life

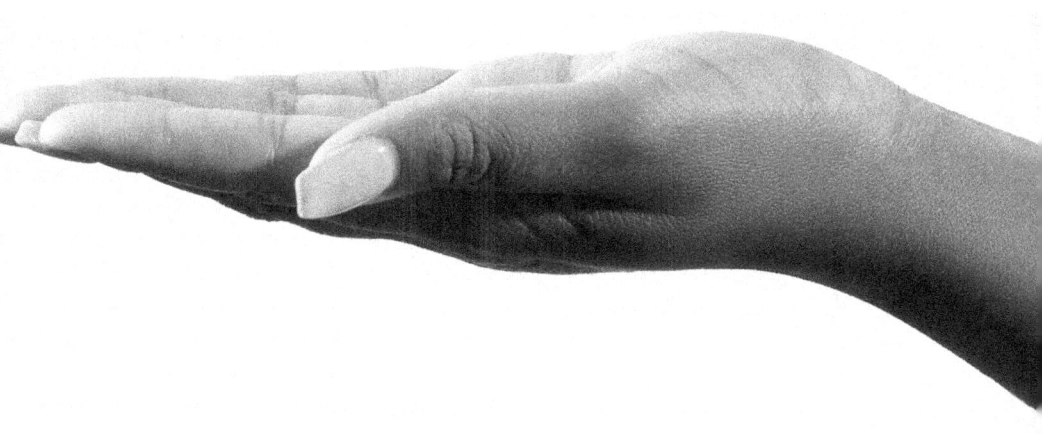

Justice

God of justice, tell me of your fairness,
Your mercy, your love.
Awaken the seed of justice you have planted within me.
You hold each man's reward in your hands.
Every matter, every work, everything done in secret is weighed
On the scales of your impartiality.
Your justice is as joy to a few
But an avalanche of terror to the wicked.
For the cause of the poor,
Awaken your sleeping giants,
Ones to whom you have given a cloven tongue,
And the rod of your truth.
Your justice is as light,
Permeating the darkness of the world.

Reign down your justice like a continual torrent.
Give me a voice for the widow, for the poor and needy,
For the captives, for the oppressed.
Mete out your justice!
Wet my conscience in the ink of your righteousness!
Let it run to my pen.
Let me write of your justice,
Echo your mercy and the plight of the oppressed.
Who will lead the cause of the commoner?

Send me, oh Great Judge!
I will write and speak of your justice,
Not iniquitous ramblings

Or what death is to the soul.
Something stinks in Denmark;
It's vinegar to my thirst.
Bring justice on the wings of the morning
And at the close of dawn.

Oh, let the wailing women cry out loud,
Let the righteous prophets speak,
Bring liberty to the captives.
His voice echoed from the whirlwind,
And then He said, "Will you go?
Write, oh writer, of my justice.
Echo freedom to the restrained.
Speak, oh poet, of my righteousness, my mercy, and my love!
Weep for the ever-present injustice.
I am coming with the reward of man in my hand."

Rain

That rain came falling on my head
On a day when my face was covered in tears,
But those tears were of joy, immense joy—
The type that buds from floating
Down the riverbanks of time and life
Like debris intent on no one bound—
Like seeing the rising of the sun and its setting,
The smell of flowers,
The chirping of a bird,
The reunion of a dog and master,
The first cry of an infant,
Cool breeze in the heat of summer,
A warm blanket in the winter.

The heavens were opened over me,
And it rained with milk and honey and ease.
I cast all my cares to the wind,
Danced in the rain, drank my milk,
And ate my honey clusters,
Because not too long ago I was a desert,
A barren land, a nagging maiden, a jilted lover,

A buffoon, a settler on the Isle of Burden,
And a needy giver.
I was a friend to my enemies and a tottering fence.
Oh, God of the open heavens, thank you for the rain!
Soak me in every drop.
I will tell of this wonder;
How you have once more made me
Into a burgeoning field.

Wayfarer

He came to the top of the hill
Thirsty, drained of will.
He covered his heart
As he approached the road's fork.

He wondered if he should go left
Or venture to the right,
Or if water flowed from a rock's cleft.
A slight grin veiled the pain of history.

His hands showed the wear and tear of his soul,
And his face withered by his despair.
He wasn't the comely kind
But washed like a battered rock by the River Nile.

He was a wanderer, a wayfarer
And his feet, the relics of ruin, of battle.
His soles bore cracks like the bark of an oak tree.
He was a pilgrim beaten by time.
He was a man whose likeness told his story.

Waiting for God

I waited for you in silence
In the quiet places of my mind,
Sometimes in chaos, in uncertainty, in fear.
I waited for you while my clothes soaked in tears
A plight brought on by an open heart.

I waited for you at the fork in the road.
I waited for you in turmoil and doubt.
I waited for you when others had left.
I expected you during the birth pangs of my disappointments.

I waited for you in the noise.
I patiently remained for you
Until my will became a stranger to me.
I waited for you when hope escaped me;
I waited for you to the point of failing myself,
While they mocked me for believing in a god,
I cannot see, one who chastises me out of love?

I waited for you in the cool of the day,
But you never came.
I waited for you when it didn't make sense,
When others blamed me for my disposition, my lot in life.

They said that you had somehow deserted me,
That you were somehow paying me back
For all my indiscretions, my secret scarlet.
Some said you were a trace of my imagination.

Like a faithful dog, I waited.
I waited; I expected you to come.
I who wear the crimson stain of death, of sin, and defeat,
Waited and hoped that one day you would come
To free me from me.
I am still waiting.

Sojourner in Babylon

The sojourner went to the judge
To ask him to raise the ruins of his broken city,
To end the pillaging, the oppression of the poor
And the outcry of the widow.
The judge laughed and told him to come back again.
So, the sojourner went back the next year
With a pocket full of sorrows,
A soul disquieted by complaint
And the burden of the poor and needy.

The judge laughed and mocked the sojourner,
And said, "Come back tomorrow."
This ruthless judge had arranged
A conglomerate of vile wretches
To be entertained by the plight of the humble sojourner.
The judge mocked the sojourner
While the others jeered him.
The crowd chanted, "From where this clown appears?"

The sojourner answered the ruthless judge and said,
"I am here to stand for the king of justice,
The justifier of the oppressed.
I have been a sojourner in this strange land.
I hear the cries of my forbears.
My heart is a reservoir of oppression,
My soul drenched in nescience;
The call for freedom burdens me.

I am the deferred hope of my ancestors,
Their abiding echoes.
I seek justice for the iniquities
That have drained my people.
Justice is coming to this land and a reward for the original sins
And the integrity of generations gone but present.
Justice is here.
Justice is now!"

Lust

Is it the hope of the bang,
Or the sound of my slang
That makes you want to discover if I got the honey, the sugar?
Was it the way I swayed down the aisle
With the lure that makes even kings go wild,
That made you want to swoop on me
Like an unwary prey?

Is it the promise of what lies ahead,
Or the daydream of me being in your bed
That made you come over
And snatched my attention like a Casanova?
Was it the unconscious longing,
Or was it the stare
Made known to you by the skimpy skirt I wear?

Is it the way I glide,
Right hip, left hip rocking from side to side
That made you want to ask me my name
And look at me crazy
Like good looks is a crying shame?
Was it the music of my dialect that shot chills up your spine
That made you want to know me and wine and dine?

Was it the trails of my perfume,
The way the light settled on my skin,
The contour of my lips,
The smell of heaven between my legs
That made your heart stop as you caught my gape?
Tell me.

Poor Man's Proverb

A troubled sea sees no rest.
A loose mouth marries holes in your pocket.
Hit a dog, and it will squeal;
Give a pig your pearls
And you'll soon have none.

A thief holds briers in his hands;
The man who doesn't play fair has hot coals on his head.
A drunken man is a talking fool;
Listen closely, for you will hear the truth.
See a man without a shoe?
Refrain from laughter,
For tomorrow your midnight might come.

Starve a dog, and it will find another home.
Close your ear to the first time someone cries wolf
Because fate is the trap of the one who deceives.
The man who carelessly makes a promise is doomed to a vow he cannot keep.

An empty cupboard is a poor man's proverb
For when it is full, he gives thanks
And eats as though empty.
The poor man has weathered both famine and plenty;
His wealth is in his faith,
His life is a Bible, a proverb.

The Quest

You set a way before me,
An untrodden path;
A course where the eagles trundle,
And where the air is clear.
You have set a path before me where few have gone,
A way for the strong.

But still, I question this journey,
The frailty of my steps, the unknown.
I want to return to what is akin to me,
Where all my possession is,
The place of my comfort and youth.
Then the wind whispered,
"Those possessions are filthy rags.
Is that where you want to return?"

The birds answered with a song that said a bittersweet goodbye.
How could I be angry at the wind, even at the birds?
I met a lonely sparrow, or so I thought,
Who said God kept him.
God, you must have a lofty sense of humor
Because I am a wasted desert and walking alone,
Yet there you are, giving a sparrow room and board.
The breeze carried a whisper that said, "Be Still."
I am still! I have stopped for a while to catch my breath.
Leave me alone! Give me back my things!
I want back my stuff! Take me back to my land!

I opened my eyes, and a brook appeared.
Oh God, was it you who opened this brook before me?
There came no answer, just an enveloping peace.

I drank water until complete, rested awhile,
And continued on the journey ahead.
Miles beyond the brook was a Juniper tree for a needed rest.
I dallied there till morning,
And was I awakened by the sparrow I had met earlier.
The sparrow gave me a penny and a caution,
"Do not give dogs what's holy!"
I then met a widow who said she was without food or kind.
She wanted my only penny and told me a frightening tale.
"Give, and you will get," she said after she had bosomed my treasure.
I saw an apple tree raided of its fruit,
It had all but two abandoned apples from a low-hanging branch.
One was rotten, the other whole.
I ate and continued on my path.
I met a dove upon rising.
It had lodged on my shoulder all night.
"Where did you come from, silly dove?"
It uttered nothing but remained with me.
The dove became my fellow sojourner on the path of truth,
On my way to the light.
I had no home, no nest, just hope of life beyond.

Black Woman's Plea

Black woman, I plead your cause!
Your moans have reached the heavens;
They saturate the clouds.
Even the skies can't hold
The weight and the burden of your tears.
They are an ever-flowing stream.

Black woman, I have asked God for justice
For everything looted, everything taken
From your alabaster box.
They seek to uproot your fortress,
Soak your wick in water,
But as if by grace, the soul of your flame still burns.

Black woman, I mourn for you,
For your children and your children's children.
Black woman, rest;
For tomorrow you will sing a new song!

Come, See a Man

I knew a man who could tell you
About things, only you and God would know.
I met a man who could tell you your thoughts
And what was written in the stars for you,
Whose breath smelled like the heavens
And whose words were like a honeycomb;
Though sometimes bitter to the ears,
But all the while, good.

People said,
"Come see a man who…"
He was a man who knew what omens lay wait
On your path through life.
He warned, healed,
And at times brought terrible news.
He showed the way to the light
And spoke nothing but the truth.
He wanted to help everyone
But couldn't help himself.
His nest was solemnity;
He had no friends but was revered by all.

Come, see a man who knows how your road will turn,
Whose ears are nested on the clouds of heaven,
Who sits and observes the stars.
For the sick, he adds a little oil and a prayer,
A word for clarity.
Some say it is necromancy or Obeah;
Others call it good.

He lost his powers by visiting a grave to save
Someone not worth being saved.
For years he sat doomed to silence,
Or was it regret over losing the eyes that saw,
Ears that heard
And a mouth that spoke;
So, in hearing, he heard nothing.
In seeing he saw nothing
And in speaking, he said nothing
Because the fire in him was quenched.

Carnival

The joker became king,
And the king, the clown.
The one who had more became the least.
The true king wore the slippers of the common man.
The ace was the holy fool.
The saint was asked to marry the harlot
And a ruthless king took a virgin as his bride.
Everyone was too raptured to notice
They were all players in a carnival.

The Upward Climb

I wish I'd met Sisyphus
As he did the upward climb
To a fate marked by the mundane,
The futility of one's actions;
And bread for labor sown to the wind.
I'd collect from him
Gems for my own journey, recompense's trek.

The upward climb is for every man.
He enters this sphere crying and leaves sleeping,
But between the beginning and the end,
He will have to make the upward climb
With the reckless abandon of a feather and the tranquillity of a sparrow.
For indeed, he will pass by green pastures,
But when he thinks it's peace and safety,
The shadow of death hunts him down.

The upward climb is a lonely road, my friend,
Cause it is there that our friends take off their masks
And where life unveils who our allies are.
But friend, do not fear the upward climb
Or the slippery slope,
For it is only at the top,
And out of the mire
That you will discover the manifest will of God.

"The upward climb is a lonely road, my friend, cause it is there that our friends take off their masks and where life unveils who our allies are."

The Prince and the King

The prince stood alone in strength,
But the king hid his frailty behind his bevy of subjects.
The prince was guided by faith.
He knew he had to strengthen his resolve,
Build his defenses, and not give place to worry
Or his enemies' schemes.

The king's enemies were both
Within the walls of his mind and his palace.
His deep worry retreated
Behind his tyranny and absolution.
Those who served him and those he pardoned hated him
But remained with him out of spite of duty.

The prince, the protector of the powerless,
Was the king of the commoner
And the love of the people, his defense;
But the king's mouth and hate became his siege
And brought on the end of his reign.

It was the prince who was always the people's king,
The one moved by the feelings of their need.
For he, too, had significant deficiencies.

Faith

Thronged to the gates of the wicked
And snared like a bird,
I stumbled to get a footing, a clear vision
Because all about me were lost,
And my view became more and more obscured.
Oh, despair became the language of my soul,
A place that once poured out hope and gladness.
My soul reeked of the vinegar of the turmoil within me.

There were vipers among me,
Whose teeth stayed open to clench my flesh.
And outside my door, ruin awaited me.
It followed me like my shadow and stayed at my heel.
Still, I saw the sun bursting over faith's horizon.
It came to dry up the muck around me.
Oh, the sun arose and brought forth its light to this cold, dense city.

Thief

Black frock thief whom the tide has led,
Whose soul's in limbo, though not dead.

You are neither foe nor dear.
You, who in obscurity fate doth tear.

The hem of your soiled garment,
The masking of your secret torments.

What does await is your harvest:
Penance for the tears cried against you.
Melancholy will reveal the weight
Of your many atrocities.

You will go to where darkness
Defies light and where man's star no longer shines.

My Faithful Friend

The stars will guide you,
When the straw breaks your back.
Only the cruel crushes a bruised reed,
But I will remember you.
I will be ever close to your broken heart.
I will listen for your faintest cry.
I will share my bread with you.
You can come to my endless supply of water
If thirst becomes your enemy.
I won't ignore the quiver of your hurting heart.

May the winds never snuff out your flame
Or calamity silence your voice.
I will plead your cause,
When you have been quieted by circumstance.
I will carry you when your burdens are too heavy.

I will catch the arrows headed for your back
And the snares laid at your feet.
And on the days, you feel less than yourself,
I will be for you what you have been for me, faithful friend.

Patchwork

"Don't patch any old cloth," said my granny when an old lover tried to come back.
"Don't lay naked before your enemies lest you are mocked," said my preacher.

When famine strikes, your friends will choose you,
And your enemies will flee from you.
They will leave to spread your shame.
They will say, "She is done! There is no hope!"

The unsuspected will cover your faults without consolation or revelation,
But those who once fed from your bosom will air your dirty laundry.

A family is like a rudder that keeps you on the right path, even in contrary winds,
A stick that is left unbroken
Even in the most boisterous tempest.

Learn to live as though money has no rule over you,
And in time, you will master money.
A man's silent foe will frighten him
More than his shadow at night.
Trust no shadow!

In the end, we are all old rags, darning ourselves with new cloth.

"A MAN'S SILENT FOES WILL FRIGHTEN HIM MORE THAN HIS SHADOW AT NIGHT; TRUST NO SHADOW!"

Mortal's Equality

An eye for an eye leaves everyone blind.
Tooth for a tooth leaves everyone mute.

If everyone seeks, who will find
The dropping left behind by a cockatoo?

If everyone gets on stage, who will watch
The baby in the cradle, grandpa's clock?

The seamstress left the cook to patch,
Priced garments made of wool and flax.

If you bring a plate to someone hogtied,
How will he eat, or do you want him to die?
You can't cover a volcano with your favorite blanket,
Hide a dog's bark or perfume stink.

Do what you must, but don't ever think
You can sow corn and, in the end, reap peas.
You get what you have already done.
The truth will emerge from obscurity on a day you would rather not have it.
The last breath is mortal's equality.

Bitter Gall

When will you let go of yesterday,
Of they and them and him and her?
Your scorn has blinded you to hope,
To sunshine and the new horizons.

Those who know you have for long
Distanced themselves from you like a plague, a shame.
You, my fair lady, is like a bitter elixir,
Bitter gall, perfumed stink, colic
After a great feast,
The debris of what was
But is long gone,
The ghosts of yesterday
Which rest in the crevices of your soul;
And the bones of disappointments and hurt.

Do you not see that life is a budding flower?
You can smell and kiss the roses,
If you cover up the thorns!

Crack in the Mask

We stare at painted faces,
But fail to behold our own reflection.
The world is the mirror on the wall,
Which lies to us about beauty.
We are stunted by perception,
And wish we could be somebody else
And live their fairy tale.
What we all fail to see is—
We all have a crack somewhere beyond the mask,
Somewhere beyond judgment.
True beauty defies perfect eyebrows,
Powdered cheeks, colored lips, and filters.
Beauty lies behind the gap in the mask.

A Friend in Adversity

I went to my neighbor's house to beg sugar
To feed my hungry child.
She told me her cupboard was empty
And to go pray,
But before she closed the door in my face,
The wind blew away her kitchen made of straw.

A stranger came my way
And fed me honey and pulses
And gave me a surplus I hadn't room to contain.
I blessed the kind, sir,
And made my way to my neighbor who had lost
Her fortune over a petty lie.

Enough is never enough to the one
With a hole in his heart and his pocket,
To the one hoarding treasures,
The elements can destroy.
My neighbor was a mange,
But I, a friend in adversity.

Room for One

Two handmaidens were in a treacherous scheme to end the other and to lay on the bosom of their woman master.
They bickered about each other to the master's amazement and sometimes bewilderment. It seems like for an everlasting that these two women camped out at a road called brawl and a street called bickering.

One maid was the bane of the other's existence, the other, salt on an open sore.
Still, the feud lingered and dragged on for nothing shy of eternity.
They brought their plight before the master, with one thinking the other was the beloved help of the ruler.
After all, they made the cold walls of the palace home and often made bread out of a stone.

One was compelled by duty, the other, loving sacrifice.
One feared and loathed her master; the other washed her feet.
The master loved the one moved by sacrifice but despised the one guided by bitter obligation.
They both cast lots with Cain to pick crumbs from the master's floor.

The Wanderer Who Wasn't Lost

I met a wanderer who wasn't lost.
He saw it as his purpose to walk from lane to lane spreading good cheer.
Gave a fed dog two bones;
While I chase away the hungry one.
I married an adulterer
But jilted a faithful man.
I gave a rib to a knave who collected a dozen
And lent my coat to a lad though he wasn't frozen.
I bargained with Paul to quickly silence Peter,
But Peter had a debt he couldn't pay Paul.
My enemy begged me vinegar,
But I offered him water from my well.
My friend slapped both my cheeks after I had given him my heart.
The fat cat ate the dog's last meal when the dog stopped to pray.
A good-for-nothing told me I had dropped my only coin,
Only to save it for the nun who buried hers in her bosom.

Wisdom

It was wisdom that led me to the light,
And faith which opened my eyes.
I had heard the call to rise higher,
To go where I had never before gone,
And to reach heights never ventured.
It was wisdom that told me
That I am never truly alone,
Not the one directing any step
I take in even places I put myself.
It was wisdom that stretched
Out its arm for me and pulled me
Close to its bosom.
It was wisdom that became my compass
When I was in the belly of the beast.
It was wisdom who fathered me
And wrapped its arms around me
When life's storms bent me.
It was wisdom that brought me peace.
It was wisdom that filled my heart with a song.
Yes, it was wisdom that brought forth
The buds of the seeds of love and joy in my heart.
It was wisdom that saved me from myself.

Chasm

He came to a fork in the road—
Hell to the right and heaven to the left,
And a chasm in the middle.
He craved hell more than peace, more than sanity
Because hell was his life.
His childhood was torment, tares, and prickly pear.
In adulthood, he chased lust
And lived a wretched life.

He found euphoria in the whorehouse,
But melancholy in his own house.
He hated the wife of his youth
But stayed out of obligation.
The wife wanted to keep up the facades
Of perfection and victory.
Her mother did; why wouldn't she?

He felt he owed her his life,
But what he didn't know was,
The wife of his youth,
Had given a mermaid a piece of his clothes
And his wedding ring in exchange for undying love.
As time went on, she saw
That he hated her the more.

She had put a yoke around his neck
To chase away the other women;
But now, the love potions had stopped working.
The silly snake wanted to carry water in a basket.

Now, he was between a rock and a hard place.
He was stuck between hell with his beguiling wife
Or heaven alone,
But he chose to stay at the outskirts of the chasm.

When Time Stood Still

I will tell you of a time when the time stood still,
When the earth, air, and sea rested,
And man looked at his reflection in the mirror,
Only to meet a stranger there.

I will tell you of a time when freedom wasn't free,
And rich and poor were made equal by time—
When things once taken for granted
Were craved and longed for.

I will tell you of a time when all men had was time
Because time became a friend held in contempt.
"Time heals all things," they say.
No, not time!
It was time that reduced men to squalor.
It was time that made his money grow tares.
Time became man's nemesis and his fears, his friends.

Part Three

NOSTALGIA

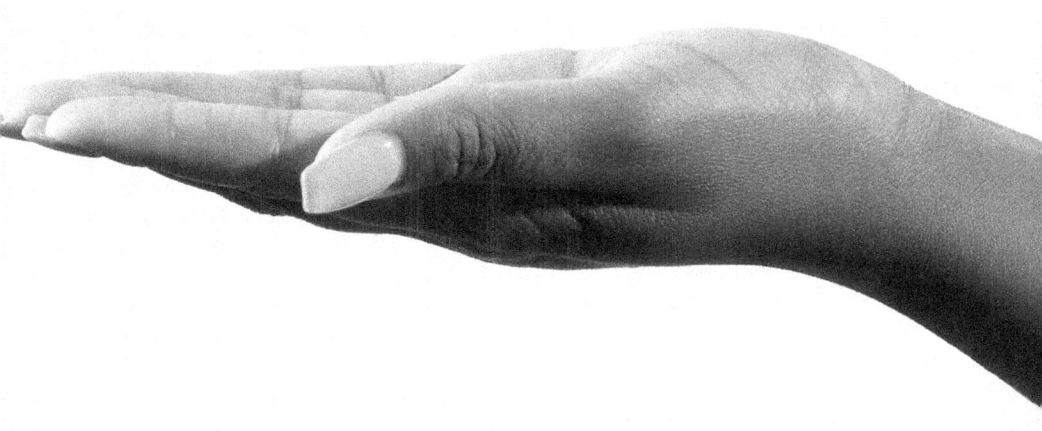

Lingering Echoes

I hear the old echoes lingering still
In the silence of my mind,
Bursting through the stillness of my quiet amnesty.
Sometimes they are as audible as the—
The piercing chirp of a miserable bird
And at other times, I
By my own doing, beckons,
These lingering old wretches to come forth.

Still, I listen, waiting for them to tug at my hem like an old maid still trapped in the passage of time,
Of being the girl who faithfully believes
Her prince charming will come, one day,
And that, of and old fishwife, still sitting outside the walls of mercy, asking God
To win back the heart of the man she chased away.

Sometimes, like an old virago,
These echoes ritually sip tea
With the other ones, the ones still hanging onto
Sugar-coated fallacies.
Sometimes I hear them stampeding through the hallways of my mind like a short-tempered salesman
Who made it ten minutes late to pick up his check.
Other times, I hear them squealing

Like a young shoat made cheerless from a hungry belly.
I am the lingering echoes of everyone I have met.
I am the smoke trails of my ancestors,
My grandmother, my mother,
My friends, my betrayers, my foes, and my teachers.

Even now, I am held captive by the subliminal
Whispers of the nursery rhyme fed to me
As a staple of my youth.
My jack fell down the hill and broke his crown,
But I destroyed it a little more;
And when it was time to put it back together,
I remembered what my granny told me about using an old cloth to darn the new,
"Don't darn new cloth with the old!"
And I ran from all the echoes that chased me.

How do I keep up with the noise?
Am I me or the noisome chorus of
The lingering echoes of the women who raised me?
Now I sit silently planning my exodus from the echoes
That pauperized the souls of women
Whose blood runs through my veins.

Should I be like Peter and deny the only thing I know,
Or should I like Judas, sell my patchwork kind of belief
Given to me by all my kinfolks for a mere thirty piece?
Still, they won't leave.
I am these haunting retorts.

Veranda

He sat there as if to let you know
He was the ruler of his castle,
The king of the kingdom, the patriarch.

His frame—etched in his seat.
From day to night, from night until the day,
He sat silently observing everyone
He could see from the veranda.

He knew who came and who left,
Who came to borrow and who came to steal.
He watched on from the capsule of the veranda.

Those who came to his courtyard
Brought respect in both their pockets and mouths.
He listened to gossips but repeated none.
He was neither friend nor foe to anyone.

"Trust no shadow after dark," he said to me,
One day when he almost got bamboozled out of a portion of his possessions.

I, too, came to learn the virtues of the veranda.
Sit and observe every player, every move
Like the playing of chess.
Take your eyes off no man or beast.
Let your intuition guide you.

The veranda was my first school.
It taught me the intricacies of human nature.

Children of Fire Rock

The hill stood insurmountably as though placed next to the sky.
At least, that's how we saw it:
Vast and beyond our comprehension.
But we were elated to go to Fire Rock.

We borrowed Sisyphus's strength
For every trek up the mountain range.
Minutes later, we were blown away
By the great hue, the magnificence of the view,
The bedecking of the tall grass
On the landscape of the mountainside.

The sugar cane summoned our taste in the heat of the sun,
As our taste buds yearned for its delight.
Even though Mr. Osmond
Would caution us about sinkholes,
The lure of the green pastures captivated us.
It had a sure pulling,
And it enveloped the well.

"The last man to the well is a loser," my brother said,
As we galloped among the cows
Set to graze in the pastures.
The one jackass laden with the day's meal
cautiously climbed the hill.
He was a faithful donkey!

Jackfruit, watermelon, and pineapple bathe our bellies,

as the freshwater quenched our unified thirst.
And when we were sated, the grass became our beds.
When it wasn't our playground,
We somersaulted down the hill.

Oh, Fire Rock,
I am in your debt for the childhood memories,
The oneness with nature
And the marvelous wonders of country living.

Rum Bar

I watched the men as they strolled into the shop.
It was the same spectacle every day:
Upward walking, shoulders erect, money in tow,
Excitement on their faces
And longing in their eyes.

Sooner rather than later, the booze sunk to their bellies, and the insatiable thirst for tranquillity arose.
They, like babies, would cry for more hush
After midnight's clock crowed, and the earth slept.

Night had taken their shame and pride,
And they knew not that they had been emptied of every penny in their pockets.
Each glass of rum dissipated caution till there was none!

I hid amongst the fixtures in the bar to listen
To tales of adventures never taken
And many other bar fib narrations.
Sometimes things went well beyond my years.
My age blinded me to the dangers of my eavesdropping, but childish glee soon informed the men
Of my unwanted presence.
As I got older, the men who ignored me
hovered over my pollen like a bee!
I scolded these old wretches and chased them away.
There would be no honey for these ruins.

Seaside

I hear the lure of the water,
The whisper of the wind.
I feel the pulling of the ocean,
The smell of the salt in the sea.

Seaside, seaside, seaside, I come alive with you!
Menaced by the stench of the angler's catch,
I hopscotched over fish scales and fish guts
As I hurried to the shore.
No better feeling than the sea breeze, the kiss of the sun,
The dancing of the waves, toes awash with sand.

Seaside, seaside, seaside, I come alive with you!
I see Sonny's boat swallowed up by shrubs,
Like fish babies still trapped in a net.

Seaside, seaside, seaside, I come alive with you!
I saw the sinkhole nestled under the sea grapes.

Not too far left and a little south of the gigantic almond tree
Which was disguised by sea moss and covered in morass
Waiting for a wandering foot.
Still, I waited to be greeted by the sun-baked fishermen coming from the ocean's deep.

Seaside, seaside, seaside,
I come alive with you!

You

I can fly without wings,
Walk in the rain as though in the sun,
Survive on water, if by fate,
But couldn't lose you without shedding who I have become.
You are water to my flower, ring on the hand of a lover.

I can walk up a mountain backward,
Only if you are there,
Sail on troubled waters,
Cross the Atlantic Ocean on foot,
But I couldn't lose you
Without losing my faith and sense of self.
You are my wisdom and logic,
And the truth that challenges me to be more.

If the devil tempted me with riches and a vast domain,
I'd choose you instead to share my cot, my single bed.

Deep Roots

I have deep roots,
Roots joined to my ancestor's hips,
Seeds seasoned by my grandmother's dreams.
I have got roots growing in the water of my conscience, spawn of the writings of my faith
And the beliefs of those gone before me.

I have got roots made to thrive in the quagmire
Of the feud between the status quo
And my stubbornness.
I have roots covered in the dirt of teachings and ideologies spoon-fed to me
By my masters' hands.
Fed?
Fed and quieted by the poisoned meat of oppression and fools' philosophy.

I have got roots deeply rooted in the American dream.
Is it a dream, America?
What of the white picket fence promised to me—
The thirty acres and a mule?

Tell me, somebody,
Have I remained in the dream I started
Before I crossed the water?
Will somebody wake up sleeping beauty
And take her back to her deep roots?

I Am She

I am she who wears the victor's crown,
The scarlet letter, the wedding gown.
I am she whose color is like the kiss of the sun.
I am she who Solomon bestowed the bounty of his treasury and the gems of his kingdom.
I am she!

I am she who sages have kissed, the kiss of life, the prophet's gist.
I am she who women begrudge,
Who made captors still by the curve of my frame,
The touch of my breasts, the move of my hips.
I am she who captivates eyes and hearts.
I am she!

I am she whom kings have sought out
To decorate their bedchambers,
To house their seed,
Seed to bring forth the harvest of the creator's design,
A masterpiece and sometimes a byword,
A crossbreed confused by its appearance.
I am she, lover, and chattel.

I am she who have passed through death's dark valley
To carry a spawn that made me cry.
I am she who stirs up passion and incites men to change
With the sweetness of my mouth,
A song of my heart,
And a little noble lie.
I am she, the harvester of the tree of life.

Homeland

I was away for quite some time,
And on my return, even familiar places seemed foreign.
I became a stranger in the place I used to reign,
My memories went senile and lagged behind time.

The pollens gave me an intruder's welcome.
There was neither an expectant fanfare
Nor a prodigal's feast to come.
Exiled was I on my birth soil
And tormented by murmurs of hard toil.

The stares of the town's people were like daggers in my back.
Someone said, "A penniless pocket doesn't warrant a welcome back."
Decadence spoke on one-time familiar faces,
Age and despair seemed to have left traces.

Men, women, and children followed the same chorus: who will help us?
I was once an outcast in the land I was born—
I was too alien, too foreign, too torn.

Dying Ember

A light used to shine here.
It had a lure so captivating,
You could almost touch it.
But there now hangs looming darkness,
Where the light used to be.
Nightfall came and stole the sun.
It brought despair, defeated laughter,
And the fire ceased to be.

Now, all that lurk are dying embers
On which the vestiges of an almost forgotten past hang.
Do we look ahead with hope to a shadowy eternity,
Or stay locked in the trap of the darkness's spell?
Still, faith revives itself and beckons belief.

She Rises

She's been told who to be,
Where to go and how to act;
And every day, she's presented with images
So foreign to her yet so captivating.
She's been through too much
To not know what moves her.
Life has taught her to be ashamed of her story,
But her story has been the springboard
For all that moves her.
It draws her to desire and the light.

Everyone has a plan for her life,
But she refuses to be suppressed by the opinions of others.

She's been told her head is in the clouds
And that she should fall back into their reality.
She is evidence that a seed can thrive
From dirt thrown on it.
Still, she refuses to be guided by an illusion
Or a false sense of self.
She remains confident in this one thing,
"God is within her; she will not fail."

Now she moves to the sound of own her beat,
Sings to her rhythm,
And flows with what has always been for her:
A love that sees beyond any limitation or mistake.
She travels light
Because life has taught her to take nothing
But an open heart and the gift of life.
And in the moments when everything is low,
She rises.

Lament

Tears in the wind,
Eyes that bear defeat,
A heart drenched in the refuse of war
That culminated at the end of impossibility;
She laments on the side of her bed
Where the sun's never been,
Where the air is stagnant,
And peace is a fleeting lover.
There's a volcano erupting within;
Whose traces are imprinted
In the corners of her eyes.
She wants to make a run for it,
But she is anchored to a familiar past.
Day-to-day, she rehashes scenes from her life
And plays house with the spoils
And laments over its players.
The sun is breaking through her cracks.
Light wants to break through the crevices
Of her black-painted reality,
But she refuses to let it in.

Peaceful Home

The world knocked at my door,
And I told it to go away.
It later returned with reinforcements
And a barrage of other devils.
Still, I refused to let them in,
So, they stayed there and knocked for hours and gnawed at my solace.
Sleep became my enemy, and peace evaded me.
I asked what they came for,
And they in unison said,
"We have come for your peace, your joy, and your energy."

These wretches tormented me for what seemed an eternity.
They camped outside my dwelling place
With offerings of tribulations and torment masked by the small foxes of my hidden desire.
They told me to close my eyes and to taste.
Even from behind the walls of my safety,
I could smell the death escaping from the cups.
Their waves of torment pushed against the fort of my sanity.

The devourers watched me,
As I got up to cast my last trouble to the wind.
"Accept our gift or die," they said.
They plagued me to fellowship with them.
I quickly realized that the more I protested,
The more they fought back.
I closed my eyes, strengthened my spirit,
And said nothing.
They left one after the other,
And peace returned to me.

Lost

If ever I get lost,
Let it be in thought.
I pray I go to places through time and space
Few have gone.
I pray I see God.
I have a few questions for him.
I pray I see both my grandfathers again
For one last hug,
One last word of encouragement,
One last kiss upon my cheek.

If I ever get lost,
Let it be among the lilies,
In a lavender field,
Among rows of anthuriums and violets.

If I ever get lost,
Let it be under the atrium where God's glory shines,
Where his essence can be felt,
And where his light will flood
This heart of mine.

Steps to Nowhere

I think I have been here before.
This is not a déjà vu.
Haven't you heard, there's nothing new?
I have been here before in this same cycle,
But only with different players and in another place.
Is this my doing, a path destiny has chosen for me,
Or something my restless soul keeps conjuring up?
What is my lesson?
Is it finding the truth, the meaning of life;
A virtue that waits on the inward man
To embrace destiny's lot?

This place is all too familiar,
And I somehow know how this will end:
All for nothing again, again.
I have been here before.
I see how the script will go.
But why am I blindfolded to what
Lies beyond the glee of my heart?
Is this my fate, failure to see the light?
It's half past midnight but noonday in my heart.
I am falling in love with the chasing of the wind,
An intimate circle, a maze, somewhere I have been before.

A Great Man

There once lived a great man, whose faith was his curse,
Who gloated over his riches,
And whose pride was a sore thumb.
In plenty, he had the best of friends,
but in adversity, a few.
He pondered if riches could save him
And if his few remaining friends would leave.
Some had sailed the seas with him in calm,
But would they stay in the storm?
His plight was only known to him
When the great gale came.

He lost everything and was stripped raw, naked;
And in his bitter plight and destruction of his walls,
He remembered what the scribe had written,
"Will a man gain the whole world and lose his soul?"
His soul was an old fort,
Looted by every vagabond who came to pillage his destiny.

His walls were breached, and strength escaped him.
And he remained in the wilderness of despair
Bound by a noose of regret
Till an unknown messenger asked him,
"What is it you seek in the graveyard?

Is it to give life to the dead, smell the stench of death,
Or take your place in an unfinished grave?
There is life beyond this death.

Come out of your doom
And call forth your soul to rise to freedom."

He arose from the ashes to eat the honey from life
And to drink its milk.
Still, like a dumb dog, he returned to his vomit
And he forfeited his dream.
I passed by his tombstone one day,
And it read, "A prudent man robs the grave;
A foolish man gives up his goods."
He gave up all his goods,
And his grave remains one of the wealthiest places on earth.

Lamentation One

She wishes she could press a replay button and live her life again, but then, how could she give up the treasures she has found amid the chaos and turmoil? She is miles farther than her wit's end but summonses the courage to go beyond all restraints. Where did the years go, the dreams, the promises? Is this her moment of truth, her fork in the road, her epiphany?

Faith beckons her to stretch beyond normalcy. She needs to open herself to great possibilities, restore her old cities, and break down the walls that have her barred in. She also needs to call on the strength to persevere and get to that place of walking on water. She must rely on a power outside her limit to change the course of her life.

She knows so much is at stake. She is aware that time is far spent. Complacency is still her most faithful companion, and fear is the bed she lies on at night. She feels change is close, yet the familiar echoes defeat. Moving forward requires that she has her reckless abandon arrested. It also asks her to assert liberty from the past and its players who have emptied her treasury. Still, she holds on to the vestiges of a crippling past.

She is chasing wisdom, but sometimes it eludes her. In stillness, her truth confronts her. The smiles of others unearth her bewilderment. The memory of a not-so-long-ago past often agonizes her. Where did the time go? Did the winds that brought the tumult into her life somehow steal time? Much of what she sees isn't real. Many of her fears are merely illusions. They are just vanities!

She must travel down a path of self-discovery. Moving down this course is all but a part of her story. She knows she must leave regrets behind or risk being sidelined. The journey looks daunting. She will have to wear many hats: a farmer because she must plant seeds if she hopes to harvest in the distant future. She will have to be a miner because there are precious gems that await. She will, above all, assume the role of a ship's captain. She will have to go down with the boat if all fails. She is determined to persevere, conquer, and win this game called life.

Lamentation Two

Look at where and what chasing the wind has brought me! I feel like a shell of what once was but is no more. I feel like somehow, I could be more, could be somewhere than here, here at this juncture of my life when all is decaying right before my eyes. When did I get to this placed called here, the place I most dread at this very minute? Where am I? I feel like many black holes have sucked me dry. I can honestly say that all my life, I have been suctioned to the point of depletion from many black holes.

They waltz into my life, knowing that they were headed straight for the kill. Little did I know I was the one who would have to clean up after the audience had gone. When did the rape and travesty of my life filled with all its potential unfold? I had pearls, the pearls of my youth, but I cast them to the swine. I had what was holy secretly tucked under the blanket of a soft heart, but I gave it to dogs to trample under their feet. Now I must scramble and shuffle for an ounce of "heart" left in me. Is there anything heart left in me?

Now, this girl cries out. She hollers. She bawls. She asks me why I had squandered my youth and had prostituted my dreams and gifts? As if answering God himself, I turned to her and said, "I don't know. I am sorry. Forgive me." She answered after a period of stillness and said, "Get my pearls! Get what was once holy and sacred from them fools, who like jokers you allowed to waltz in this once-thriving courtyard. Find me!" She convicted me with a kind of conviction that didn't reduce me in size. I was already living a lie: big on the outside but so minute on the inside. The dam that used to be here is an old dried-up riverbed, pirated of all that is good and blessed. She hollered. She bawled and said, "Rescue me, you slave trader! Why are you asleep while pirates and thieves lurk outside your door seeking what is good and holy?"

I listened as a child being scolded and said, "Help me get up. Help me out of this sleep I have been living." She answered calmly but somewhat sternly, "Take up your bed and run!" I sat there, crippled momentarily from the reprimand.

Still, something leaped within me, and before I set out to walk, something took hold of me, and I leaped forward and flew into my destiny. I went back to the thieves and pirates for my booty. I took back my chests laden with jewelry, and then I found what was left of my pearls.

I walked up and down the marketplace looking for "promise," then in a still small voice, I heard her say,
"Here I am leaning on the arms of wisdom. My wings are trampled and somewhat broken." I grabbed them both. I placed "promise" on my bosom and wisdom on my heart. I took them back to the young woman who cried out, but she was long gone because I had returned from sleep. Her work was done.

Marketplace

The marketplace was spirited, with characters flooding the walkways. They corralled the food stands like ants and fat. The smell of food and liquor filled the air as patrons rounded up to wet their palates. I heard peanut carts whistle and the hum of every hungry belly. They stood in line for a taste of Mass Jerky's barbecue chicken and seafood soup with fresh pepper on the side. Extra was the server's nightmare, a reality made known by their sour faces. At the counter is Percival or Mr. T watching over his poker table lest any sticky finger person dares let trickery get the best of them. Len was the chief musician, a title bestowed by himself. He used music to taunt the crowd and to throw stones from his glass house. Both retribution and targeted bullets would prove that his house wasn't impenetrable from rocks. There were also "mouta massies"[1] in the marketplace. It behooved the others to draw figs lest their nakedness was exposed.

Then some plotted to rob and to kill you; not a real sort of death but the death of a dream, of sanity, of peace and moral obligation.

What remained were the sages, those whose spirit, vision, and words guided the chosen; the babes and suckling also came to the marketplace on their guide's arms, chest, and shoulders. The babes came to feed and to suck nectar from the Tree of Life. The spectators were the last to leave the Quadrangle, their nest and cocoon. Year in, year out, they looked at others to affix both their attention and mouths and reveal what they had found.

---

[1] Mouta massie is a Jamaican colloquial term for a person who spreads rumors.

"Draw figs lest your nakedness be exposed."

Ocean of Tears

His soul was a wasted desert, a dunghill.
He languished in pain from a longing heart,
A heart that was uninhabited land;
Yet oceans of tears pour out from his parched soul.
He'd waited for his morning,
But it hadn't come.
He had seen nights darker than the hours before dawn.
Life had brought on angered distress, a famine.
At night, his drought became washed
With the sweat of anguish, lingering sorrow.
His heart was bitter, his soul a desert, but his spirit an ocean of tears.
Day in, day out, he bottled the tears to quench an endless thirst.

With Wings

Fly above soldier boy.
Kiss the clouds,
Gather the stars in your hand,
Ascend into the heavens,
And hug the feet of he who sent you.
"Welcome home, good and faithful servant.
Leave your wings here.
Those were only for the journey.
This way to the crown," a booming voice said.

You are somewhere in heaven smiling now,
A smile that was seen on earth as a shining star.
You didn't pass the cup.
You poured everything out for those who came to drink.
Now, you are in paradise awaiting the messenger's robe.
Tell God I said, a well-deserved robe.
Your shift left a pulse too powerful not to have been felt.
Why are prophets celebrated after they are gone?
The show, my friend must go on.
Now we know there's truly a treasure in every earthen vessel.

Life is Strange!

Hearts beat and faint in despair for a world in travail;
A world where truth is in hostility to darkness.
Hearts beat and faint in despair
Over a kingdom where the joker became king,
Where the least became the chief
And the first became the last.
Hearts beat and faint in distress over uncertainties and perplexities,
Over tumult and strife in the inward man,
Over the loss of will and courage.

Life is strange!
The mouth which curses is the mouth that utters praise.
The wind which brings the scent of spring
Also causes the fire to spread.
To escape the madness,
We get lost in fantasies
And be consumed by the plot.
We become each character to escape the madness of our world and repeat their lines,
To live in their moment
And feel their joy and covet their lives but only for a reprieve from our plight.
Life is strange!

Make Room

She waited for the rain, but it never came to water the hope of a flower, which refused to bud. It wasn't that she hadn't given the bulb a chance to grow. It was the flower's refusal to see that it could bloom from its ruins. She remained stoic at the thought that what she had sown could not bear fruit. She existed either on the hem of hope or that of despair. Still, she watched to see if, even at her whispers, the flower would bloom. So, every morning, her tears would water what she had planted years before deferred hope had set in.

Then one day, the earth spoke to her and said, "Make room, you barren woman. For not too long, you will reap the harvest for which seeds you have sown." She wanted to believe that maybe she had heard wrong. That maybe her inner voice had become boisterous; that perhaps it was just her mind. So, she remained in gloom over a life which had yet to see bounty, and she sobbed. After she had cried, her soul wept bitterly. She met an onlooker who uttered the words she had heard but dismissed, "Make room, you barren woman. For soon, the childless will bring forth fruit from her womb."

"I can't be hearing this," she said in disbelief. Still, the stranger repeated the words once more and disappeared from her presence. She pined over the words she had longed to hear but quickly dismissed them as figments of her mind. Days later, as she journeyed to see the widow, she occasionally traveled to visit on Sundays, she found a scroll along the path. It read, "Hard ears eat stones. Ignore the omens and repeat your lessons. For out of nothing, something will come." The warning echoed in her soul and left a burden too hard to carry. Still, she continued on the gravel path to see the widow. As she made it to the wooden door, she dried her tears then knocked on the door. A weakened woman opened the door and exclaimed, "Good to see you, my child. Come on in."

As they sat down to tea, she said, "Next year, this time, you will bring forth seed." She listened intently to the widow and took a moment of silence. Now, she believed her wish was coming true. The widow anointed the young woman's head and her feet and prayed for her that every angel at her disposal would guide her.

After the meal was over, the two women embraced, and the younger departed. The young woman gave birth to "promise" and dedicated its fruit to God in months to come.

Sitting

"Are you going to remain fixed in your chair?" she said to me. "Wake up and smell the roses. Dance to the sound of the wind. Lock eyes with the sun and ask the breeze not to whisper your secrets to anyone but God. Are you going to sleep your life away while refusing to sun your pillow of tears? It's noon, and your boudoir has grown weary from the weight of your burdens. Only if your bed could cry out and ask you to wake up from your slumber! It's still day. Make hay! Life is friendly to the dreamer, the one who takes it by the loins and binds its feet to theirs. Sitting at the edge of the river won't cure your leprous stains.

Get in and be washed by the strength of the streams. Dip your head seven times, my lady; one time for each lover who has jilted you at the altar; and when you have finished your bath, raise your hand to the heavens and thank God for a new dawn. Don't just sit there by the riverbanks, hoping someone will give you a splash.

We are no one's keeper, my friend. Haven't you heard that no one is your guard, and only a few will prove to be a friend in adversity? Pick up your jaws, laying miserably at the sea of plight, lest the whale of distress swallows you. While you are sitting, burdened by the weight of your misery, hope becomes an absconder, a fleeting lover in search of fresh honey, a new nest.

The enemy within is more in number than the enemy without. Who lights a fire on the outside of a cabin while it's winter inside? Are you still sitting there, at the enemy's table, waiting for your foul to come home to roost? Are you still waiting for a forgotten lover wearing wedding clothes and carrying a decayed bouquet? What of hope that lies beyond the veil of your blindness?"

Barefoot Prophets

"Prophets don't live here anymore," they said,
As if to force my acquiesce.
"All the prophets are dead.
I will show you where they rest," said another.
On my way to Garvey, I passed Seville Blue.
It reeked of and had a pull of oppression.
The souls of the natives cried out to me,
And they asked me to uproot
And throw into the sea
The relic of Captain Colon.
I went to seek out this intruder.
He was standing in glory;
A glory he robbed from the people of Xaymaca.
I walked to the place where Marcus grew up.
He was immortalized on a sculpture
That only bore his head;
Hidden like a candle under a bushel.

I felt him in the air, trekked his forgotten path,
And walked barefoot and listened for his echo.
The wind brought me his message on its wings.
I was guided to a place
Underneath a Seville orange tree,
And as I approached the cool shade,
I felt an unction to untie my sandals.
I obliged and entered in.
Written in the concrete below my feet were the words, this way.

I then heard a whisper that said,
"Up, up, you mighty and strong.
Why look for the dead?

Am I not in the stories told to you by your forebears?
Am I not in the quiet revolution of your soul?
You have work to do while it's still day.
You are now compelled to compel.
Provocation is the poet's bane.
The prophet, the saint, and sages speak; the poet writes.
The mantle is yours.
Will you use it? Will you be the mouth for the mute, the ears of the deaf, and the legs for the lame?"
I nodded and journeyed on, but I heard a voice telling me to go to Nine Mile to feel Nesta somewhere in the distance.

"Show me where Nesta lived," I said to a little old lady carrying a lamp along a beaten-down dirt road. She pointed to a place beyond the trees. It was light out, but she cradled a lamp. I sat where Nesta sat, and then he came with the winds. "Who is he who enters this holy hill?" It's me with the mantle Garvey gave me to take to you. He said to trim it and add oil as though a lamp. I have been summoned to a place called Revolution, where the prophets and scribes before me went. Nesta stretched out his wand and bid me come. He said, "Go to the mountaintops and in the valleys below to declare love, to speak from the heart of him who sent you, and to spread love and peace. Repair the breach and build up what the pirates and lying prophets destroyed."

This Thing Called Life

I wish my mother had told me what to expect, how life would be, but you see, she was a mute. My granny, who mothered me, tried to tell me in her way, but it took up to now to understand what she was trying to teach me. When I asked my granny what life was, she responded with a proverb that said, "A baby pig asked its mother why her snout was so long, and the mother replied, 'You are getting old. One day you will understand.'" I am still trying to understand what Granny meant.

I wish the man who raised me as his daughter had told me more about this thing called life, but all he said was, "Ignore the boys. Take up the books. You have a great future ahead of you. Make hay while the sun shines."

I wish I had listened to my school teacher who told me, "You are a smart girl. Don't get swallowed up by the world. Think before you act." Teacher, I wish I could tell you that not only did the world swallow me up, but it spewed me out more times than I can count.

I wish I had listened to my spirit when it told me, "Stop, listen, don't miss the signs, or you will come back this way again and again." I missed the signs because I didn't stop to look, and I made circles in places I was only meant to visit once.

I wish I had listened to that unassuming lady who struck up a conversation with me in a public bathroom. She said to me while she gently touched my right hand, "You are carrying burdens that don't belong to you. Let them go. Be free!" I remember every word spoken by my guides. They have become a chorus that never ends. They linger to remind me that life always rewards; it's karmic. You either fix it or repeat it.

Now I tell myself what I think I know about this thing called life.

Life can be beautiful but know that you are where your choices have led you. Many guides have been sent to you; you might have ignored them. You have even evaded the spirit within you, which leads you into all truths. Life will get messy, and people will come and go. Life gets ugly, but the beauty of it outweighs the bad. It may sometimes run short, but the blessings are immeasurable.

Part Four

The Mind of the Poet

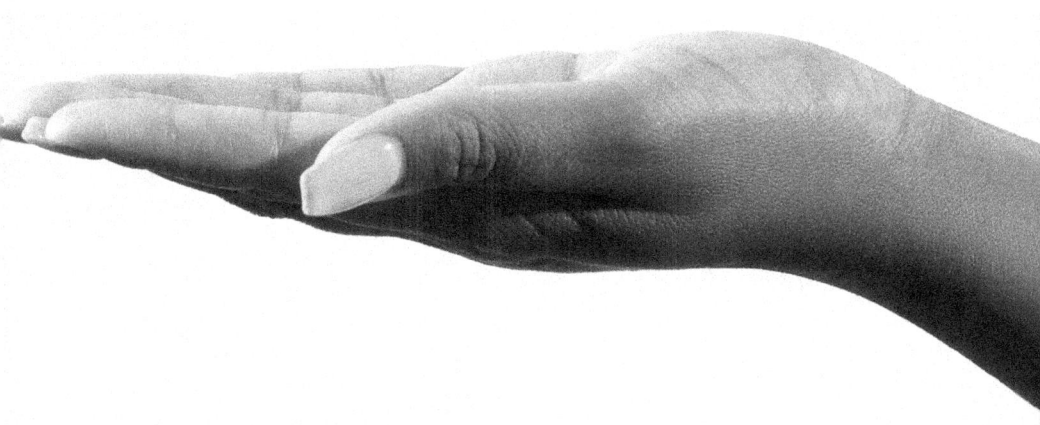

One More Race

I sat on a chair in the park, thinking of the valleys
I had been in and how I got there.
I thought about the mountains that stand before me
And the faith I need to cast them into the sea.
I have been in valleys, in sunken places too deep to see any light.
I have fought for stillness in quicksand
And only saw peaks in my mind.
I have carried burdens too heavy to expose;
I have nursed my shame and pitied my regrets.
I have faked a smile while I was dying inside
But too afraid to ask for help
Because the times I did, I was marred by opinion and gossip.
Oh, hope, you been my life raft in the most violent of life's storms.
I had held onto faith when it was the worst choice.
I have been bent past my limits, been pushed
And tossed by the waves of my disquieted soul,
But from my soul's dark crevices,
Hope beckoned me to take just one more step,
Wait one more day, run one more race.

Goodnight, Pillow

Goodnight, Pillow, we meet again.
You are the resting place for my head and heart,
The sweet refrain from the noise of the world,
My amnesty from the coupe of guilty pursuers who lay wait to ambush the quiet within me.

Oh, Pillow, drenched in the waters of a heart most burdened with grief,
A heart made bankrupt by my lofty choices, a heart on life support.
Oh, Pillow, I owe you a debt I cannot pay.
A debt as expansive as the seas and deeper than the oceans deep.

Oh, Pillow, you are the recorder of my burdens, the emblem of shame.
You keep my inadequacies, my wantonness of the mind.
Goodnight, Pillow, until we meet in the morning
When I must part with you till night.
I go to dream until I return to the madness of the world.

Who Created this Poet

My mother nurtured the seed my father gave to her,
But it was God who wrought me from dust,
And who wrote poet behind my name in the Great Scroll.
He, levied coals of fire on my conscience,
So that my mouth is unfettered, unbridled.

Who created this poet?
Was it the metamorphosis of life experiences
Filled with misery enough
Or was it the knottiness of society's woes,
The plight of the poor
Or the shadows of oppression
Inscribed in the peripheral of my inner sanctum?

The one who created this poet also placed the pen in her hand.
The heart breeds the poem,
But the pen bleeds the ink of the poet's mind.
I am poem, symmetry, rhythm, and rhymes.

Winter's Clutch

Winter came one day
When I had returned to my friend his coat.
My enemy too came that day, to see,
Perhaps to peruse, to gloat over my misery,
But he left me with his cloak.

Yes, he was defrocked and emptied of his cloak, his compass,
His eyes, his candle.
My nemesis walked away naked.
Naked!

It was winter in my house when he came,
But summer when he left me.
Did he not need his eyes to see,
His compass, his candle for direction?
Why give your foe your treasure
And cast your pearls to swine?
For winter will surely strike again.
It won't always be autumn, spring, or summer.
My enemy was an illusion, a figment of false reality.
My enemy was me—a discovery made known
By winter's stifling clutch!

The Famine of My Soul

In the famine of my soul came a tremendous tumult,
The darkest night, the longest drought,
The harshest tempest, the loudest wind.
Laughter was absent in the famine of my soul.
Even light absconded as darkness flooded the nooks and crannies of my being.

But in the famine of my soul, I found myself
Nesting by the Pool of Bethesda,
And waiting for a push, a hand to help.
No good Samaritan came,
And I devolved into worn-out rags,
So, in despair, and against all the odds,
Came an unfamiliar sound.
"From where came this sound?
From the King's mouth?" my soul asked.

In the famine of my soul, I awakened to the light,
To the noonday sun, to deliverance
To the me who was hiding from my soul.

Condemned by My Tongue

I was condemned to a life I hated,
By a sentence, I professed out of my mouth;
The same lips that kissed were the same from which guile flowed.

My tongue uttered sweet praises,
But it gave spikenard to them who came with thirst.
My murmurings and disputing exiled me
From my Canaan, from my milk and honey.

I spoke myself into oblivion by my gist, by a loose lip and an unbridled tongue,
A volcanic wave of death—
But I met a fairy who handed me a lump of coal
And said it would cleanse me and
Lighten up the burden of my soul.

I said to him, "What is your name, kind sir?"
"Jeremiah. The unspoken language of your heart sent me."
"Use the coal Judas and save your neck," said the man I knew not.

Juniper Tree

A fallen leaf was spread out in the sun,
Awaiting resurrection.
It bowed in prayer and held the promise of hope hostage.

It was sheltered by the glorious Juniper tree
Whose branches were outstretched as if to worship.
Oh, Juniper tree, the heavens drop dew on your branches
And open to give you drink.
Oh, Juniper tree, your roots cascade to meet the waters of the River Nile.

You increase in depth and breadth,
Growing like a cedar in Lebanon.
Oh, sweet Juniper tree,
Oh, how I love your shelter in the heat of the day,
And the rustling of your leaves.

Finders Keepers, Losers Weepers

I found what others overlooked;
They were stones, not gems.
Often, they were rocks in the eyes of others
But charms for me to use for my journeys ahead.
Sometimes I got things I didn't deserve.
Someone lost, but I somehow gained.

I learned to treasure morsels and to despise pleasures.
I found a treasure in a deserted place,
Carried water in a basket and spilled none, none.
I treasured a rock as though a gem,
And I hid a dime as if it were a treasured find.

I learned to treasure morsels and to despise pleasures.
It's not the what's for keeps that grounds us,
That makes us walk with the common touch;
It's the circumstances that bring us to the keeps.

Fat Cat

Fat cat, don't you ever get tired of eating?
When will you get out of your gluttonous stupor?
Fat cat, do you ever get full?
When will your insatiable thirst quench?

Fat cat, do you ever get tired of sitting on your rump,
While others work hard and slave for you?
Fat cat, have you no heart?
You have bottled the sun while it's dark everywhere else.

Fat cat, does your heart even beat like mine?
Does it get stirred by my plight and my pain?

A Black Man Was Lynched Today

A black man was lynched today, another one!
Another father, son, or friend is gone.
Click, click, boom, boom!

Somebody's mama must buy a black dress now,
A casket or maybe a box,
But only if there is money in the till,
Cause times are hard, and the struggle is real!

Somebody's wife will sleep alone tonight,
But not because her husband is an adulterer.
He's instead lying in a morgue tonight.

A black man was lynched today;
Murdered in these streets
And taken out by a light bullet.
Tell me, dear murderer,
Did your heart stand still
While you expired the life of a black man?

You can wash them with bleach,
But the blood won't leave your hands.
Will, you sit for tea happily,
Or will your conscience starve you?
Will you have eggs while his wife or his lover consumes tears?
Will you go home to sleep like the rest of the world
When a black man was lynched today?

A black man was lynched today
While some were busy burying their angst;
And while others were abandoning their humanity
To bicker over natural rights imprisoned by superiority.

Everybody shut up!
A black, brown man was killed in the streets.

Pseudo Me

Sometimes I am half the person I want to be.
Other times, I wish I was the person you want me to be,
The one others are or their pseudo-reality.

I sometimes get stuck living in perception:
The place the world lives,
So, I put on false airs to appease many for a sense of belonging,
For a pass to fit in with the crowd.

I get pulled in by their lust and enchantments,
Live in their made-up world
As I navigate through the lives of strangers
With my index finger or my thumb.

I punish my psyche, burden my mind,
And live momentarily in a daydream that brings on perception fatigue.

When I wake up out of society's slumber,
I am half of me, a pseudo me,
The me who has morphed into a cookie-cutter me,
A me who is a pinch of me.

Sometimes I try to muster enough me to get me
Through the status quo, the rat race, the never-ending
Nothingness of the farce we call life.

Sometimes I want to be someone else,
At least for a little while,
To dream someone else's dream,
To walk in someone else's shoes,
To carry someone else's cross.

But will I be satisfied to walk their mile,
Talk their talk and live their lie?
Then something within me shouted as though to teach me that
I am where I should be.

Doctor Jekyll Hide Me

Coming out like rats and roaches
And encroaching on the territory of my mind,

My principles and my beliefs;
You frighten me with your tug-of-war morality.

Oh, Doctor Jekyll, hide me.
But how can we exist in the same space,
Same grid when we are distant strangers joined by obligation?

Oh, Doctor Jekyll, hide me.
Sometimes you grant me some reprieve.
Sometimes you take an exodus.
Other times you return to drive me to the edge,
Then mock me as I hang on the scaffold of my shame.
You taunt me with your rhetoric of truth and reality.

Oh, Doctor Jekyll, hide me.
I woke up on the right side of morality.
Still, like a raging bull, you throw a volcanic tantrum,
Forcing me to abort my calm,
The small fraction of serenity I've found.

Oh, Doctor Jekyll, hide me.
Now, I am vacuumed in this darkness,
Devoid of light and knowledge,
I remain numb to any semblance of morality I was breastfed.
Oh, Doctor Jekyll, hide me.
Who can save me from this demise?
What will be the antidote for the venom which has poisoned the truth within me?
Will the day come when the duel between faith and reason end?
Will I survive without wounds?
Oh, Doctor. Jekyll, hide me!

This Poem

This poem is for every little girl dreaming of a better tomorrow,
For every youngster drawing make-belief worlds
To escape their current reality.
This poem is for the street-side vendors,
The carpenters, graveyard diggers,
Cookshop owners, corner shop proprietors,
The lady of the night,
Working to make a dollar.
This poem is for the ganja or food farmers,
The house cleaners, the janitors,
The honest hustler, the village lawyers, teachers.

This poem is for every head cook and bottle washer,
Every village that raised children it never bore.
This poem is for the chief elders, the forebears,
Every barefoot prophet.
This poem is for the ones under siege in the land of their birth.
This poem is for the conscious,
For the man whose conscience is a cleansed mirror.

This poem is for those who pass on the divine truths,
The universal song, the rhythms that move our souls.
This poem is for the preservers of our heritage,
The rastaman, the herbalist, the nonconformist, the vagabond.
This poem is for the free thinkers, challengers of the status quo,
The tailor, the midwife, the brave.
This poem is for the melanin or honey-colored queen

Covered in layers of shea butter and not bleach.
This poem is for the little girl
Who wants to wear her hair in an afro

And rub cocoa butter on her skin.
This poem is for the man who never has to rob his rib to live.
This poem is for the ghetto "yutes" and the ghetto soldiers.
This poem is for the women holding up the shoulders of their kings,
Steaming that quinoa and making that veggie stew.
This poem is for the thought provocateurs,
Who are refraining from buying
Into the ensnarement of the status quo.

This poem is for the non-economical slaves
Who refuse to bury their gifts.
This poem is for the angler who casts his net over many waters.
This poem is for the Mighty race bound in systemic chattels.
This poem is for those who don't like sloth
And those who don't compromise the truth.
This poem is for the lone warrior, the non-corrupt leader.
This poem is not for no "rassclaat" fool!

Life Support

She boasts of her opulence
And speaks loudly of her grandeur:
Amethyst sidewalks, cushioned pavements,
And flowery footpaths.
She ingrains her traditions of substance into the hearts of men from far and wide.

She beckons strangers to come and feast
At the king's banquet and to sip on aged wine.
She then implores them, the foreigners
To have no thought for tomorrow but to feed today's lust.

She invokes them to come on a promise,
But can a promise be so strong
That it pulls you to an unknown world
And forces you to forget yourself, relics of your legacy, your tongue?

She's sold strangers hope on life support,
Not a deferred hope, a dying one
Of everything which they knew before;
And all that made them divinely unique.

Sooner rather than later, they would know
That would be the thing they had to give up
For the fallacy of equality and hope;
A hope comatose and held on life support.

Dark Night's Travail

When you are in your dark night's travail,
Think it not funny to never hear
The whisper of a console from friends;
To never get a hand to hold onto,
A shoulder to lean on or a kind word spoken.

Be not frightful of the terror of the night.
It's often better than a broken vow,
The hiss of a hidden enemy,
The sting of a very faithful friend
Who once bathed your bosom in tears.

Believe it not strange to have people
Look on in dismay like some plague
Has come upon you to consume what they
Thought you beheld in your bosom.

Wish them a fair goodbye for in time, you will know
That even a loyal dog will one day bite the hand of the master who fed it.

Chance

If by chance or grace I am still here,
I'll gladly submit to fate's command,
Accept the hand I have been dealt
And wait until life reshuffles my deck of cards.

Even in valley crossings and as hope fades,
I will hang onto summer's hem
Cause then, I will look into your gaze
To see if you are for me or with them
Who seek to bring about my quietus;
The bastards who broke their vows.

Was that chance or punishment for the ones I had left?
Ones who I grew weary of long ago.

Joker's Taunt

To me, you are a shadow that appears
Without the chance of apprehension.
You bring with you a force that tears
My belief and hope past recognition.

You bring me low in the depths of Sheol—
To laugh at me like a joker's taunting,
A hungry lion perched next to a foxhole
Unknown to a silly prey while flaunting.

You bring me back into your sweet embrace,
Only to leave me standing yet again,
Fleeing in the dead of night without a trace.
I grimace at your one fatal stain,
I remain hinged to hope of sunny skies,
Waiting now in silence as despair dies.

Baby Girl

Baby girl, what's the color of your soul?
If it has a scent, does it smell like dew, rosewater, or apple cider?
Is the color bold or lightly hued?
Is it empty, dull, or uninviting?
Honey chile, what is the state of your heart?
Is it warm, cold, or on the sunny side?
Does it sing a welcome or bark an adieu?
Does it have sunflowers and grape vineyards?
Baby girl, how much do your eyes weigh?
Do they carry the weight of your world,
Or do they travel light?
Do they point me to your heart,
Or will they make me run and hide?

Squeeze

How did you pay for that?
Did you rob and steal for that?
Did you run games for that?
Have you been tricked or treated for that?

Did you sweat, lose sleep for that,
Study hard, grind for that,
Pimp, squeeze, shuffle for that?

Did you use your hips for that,
Turn tricks for that; lie for that
Or did you beg for that?
Did you give your soul for that?

Did you kill for that? Wielded a gun for that?
Did you scam for that or give your rib for that?
Did you get your forty pieces for that?
What did you lose for that?

He

He gave life and had it broken,
As friends stood still with words unspoken.
In silence, they cried rivers,
But in public, he was shadowed in quivers.

"Do you know this man?" they asked.
Too many people thought he was a farce.
In life and death, he did proclaim,
"Yesterday and today forever the same!"

Walk My Own Mile

I have walked alone while standing in a crowd;
I have loved when I have been hated,
And have given more chances than I have been afforded.

I have decided to walk my own mile,
Take my chances and be my crowd.
I will steer myself with hope's rudder
And fly on the wings of tomorrow;
And if life doth grant me grace
To fulfill my greatest dream,
I will do it alone if I have the will.

This Way Again

"This way again?" the sojourner lamented,
Thinking he hadn't been this way before.
Still, he saw the omens of his previous expedition
And his past life at a moment's notice.

"This way again?" asked the wandering dog,
Who wanted to leave its master's dwelling,
Only to find its way back home.

"This way again?" asked the jilted lover
Whose father had once again paid a dowry
For a flickering hope of eternity to Houdini.
If you don't learn your lessons well,
You will someday travel this way again.

Green Leaf

Shaded by the alpine tree,
And nestled in the forest's cocoon,
You are bathed in soft dew and fed by the sunshine.

Green leaf, you are adorned with raindrops
And glisten as though you were a diamond.
What you don't see is that the enemy of nature
Is within itself waiting to delight in your beauty.
It births and destroys,
Captivates men's hearts and leaves them in dismay.

Green leaf, I will sit by the pond and gaze at you
Before autumn comes—
And sweeps you away like trash.
I will hold onto the memory of the time I beheld
You in original splendor
and the moment you seized my heart.

Today

I woke up this morning topsy turvy,
Thinking of all that lies ahead:
The dreams, the hopes, and the wins;
The new people I will meet,
And those whom I'll bless.

I thought of the miles
I have yet to travel, sometimes alone,
The disappointments and the cries.

I then pondered the downs fate will conjure up;
But then you whispered in a reassuring voice,
"It's a new day! Life will go on."
I immediately stopped to relish
The thought of what you will bring me:
New journeys, laughter, and goodwill,
Changing courses of life and time,
Mistakes healed by the hand of God,
Collisions with fate, dreams fulfilled, and love.
Yes, love!

I am humbled that life hasn't shown me its exit yet;
And that I have the freedom to be, to hope,
To dream, to know I am guided,
And that I have made it to this day!
Today is my friend.

Thoughts

You are my celebration, my liberation,
My bittersweet journey!
I sat alone in my corner, reminiscing about the roads
I have trekked,
Victories won; battles lost.

How you must be bursting at your seams with

The weight of my thoughts,
Bothered by the ink which fills your pages.
You are so much of my soul.
You carry me!

Now, you are tied to me. You are joined to my hip.
I am so that you exist.
I can't part from you now
Until your bell chimes, or I cease to be.
You sometimes appear as a glimmer of light,
Evading my restraint.
Sometimes, you flood my mind with illusion,
Bias, doubt, and sometimes hate.
At other times, you are vanity too grand to measure.

Summer

If summer were an eternal shine,
And autumn a temporal shade,
With Christmas, winter would decline,
And spring would remain a shadow's fade.

Girl with the Kinky Hair

The fairy kept leaving her a comb,
Or so she thought.
Not a dollar for her tooth,
But a comb tucked under her pillow!

Each time the comb would be far prettier than the last.
She pondered why a comb and not a candy cane
Or a bonnet made of silk.

She summoned her pixie, and it quickly came.
"Loving fairy, I usually don't ask for much,
But I have lost a tooth again
And haven't been given a single penny.
I hope you have time to tell me
If, perchance, you did forget,
To leave me my dollar
Each time I lost a tooth.

Why did you leave me a comb while I was in slumber's nest?"
The kind fairy replied,
"Each time I came, I saw an angel bringing you
Your answered prayers.
He told me you had once more broken a comb while fixing your hair.
He said he came quickly
Because of your silent cry
And for another little girl who had been praying
For the girl with the kinky hair.
If an angel comes to your bedside before a fairy,
The fairy must then leave
And return another day;
 So, when I return,
I will carry all the dollars
I have for you, oh girl with the beautiful kinky hair."

If We Should March

If we should march this time,
What would be our cause?
Would we march for love,
The disenfranchised, the nobody, those left behind?

If we should march down another street,
Which people would be our cause,
The poor and needy, the pious, the rich?
Will it be for the shapers of the status quo, who?

If we should march today,
Who would we help,
Little children crying, old folks who've been forgotten;
People with an unknown tongue, strange taste?

If we should march on the world's stage,
How would we choose our words?
Would they bring life and yield to truth,
Or would we remain frozen by silence?

Afro Queen

Jewel of the Nile,
Who can compare to thee?
To me, you are a beacon atop a hill,
Starlight shining from the heavens,
The Milky Way, Stargate to the universe.

You are the passageway to earth and beyond,
Daughter of the sun,
A black rose whose thorns curtsy
When touched with love.
You secrete melanin
And add colors to the canvases of men.

You are God's crowned jewel,
His delight, a channel for his seed.
Dark berry, you infect your brood
With the hope of happiness and freedom,
And mourn when liberty is withheld.
You are as vast and as beautiful as En Gedi,
An abundant spring, an oasis.
Afro Queen, none can hold a candle to your light!

Pen

He went to war clothed in armor
That felt like shackles—
Sword in hand,
Shield just at his waist,
A breastplate to cover his heart,
A helmet for his head
And covers for his feet
Lest someone tries to pierce his shins
Or cuts at his Achilles heel—
But when I go to war
I am a camel through the eye of a needle.
I go in and through my mind
I go to war with my pen;
I go to fight to the echoes of my ancestors.
I go to war with the pulse
Of Mosiah, Muta, and Maya.

I go to war girded with the rhythm
And the song of a revolution not televised.
I am a silent revolution, a poet.
I go to war with my pen.
Oh, mighty pen, you give me the courage of kings,
The vigor of a thousand gladiators,
The might of Samson, the wisdom of Solomon.

Oh, I am peace, but my pen is for war.
I war for every disenfranchised youth,
Every revolutionary without a voice.
I am my pen, the effector of change,
The provoker of thought!

Guilty Pursuers

My enemies conspired against me.
They sang a chorus that it wouldn't rain on my house,
But fate torpedoed and sent me a plentiful shower.
They compromised every truth I've spoken
And maligned every inch of my character,
But my integrity silenced every foe,
Every illegal intruder of the terrain of my soul.
Oh, my soul was a sunken refuse
Of a voyager which kings once journeyed aboard.
They came from every side to accost me
And snuff out my light,
But my soul did arise from the depths of destruction
And reclaimed its place next to my spirit;
But only after my mind summoned it to escape from Sheol,
Where the gatherer of dead bones was preparing my seat.
My soul did arise and broke the bonds
And shackles of my blood-guilty pursuers asunder
And after the war was over, my soul was won.
All that remained was chaff after the high wind had passed.

Black Man Arise

Oh, black man, arise,
In your kingly character.
Oh, black man, get up,
Stand up for your right
To be equal to all but God.
Oh, black man, be strong, as Samson's might.
Oh, black man, be wise. Retreat and fight another day.
Oh, black man, do you not know,
Can you not see that the stars bow down to your rising?

Can you not tell of the promised land
God has painted on the canvas of your soul?
Oh, black man, take dominion over your heart
To conquer the issues of life.
Who was there but you
When you mapped out the path of the stars
And ran circles around the world?
You tattooed the rocks with your likeness,
And inked hidden knowledge in the spirit of your people.

Oh, black man, awake from your slumber,
Roar, shout, and illuminate every nook,
Every cranny of this earthly domain.
Oh, black man, ascend into the heavens
And touch the feet of God;
It is like the hue of your skin.
Oh, black man, you are king;
Arise to the light of your calling.

The Living Poet

Who said all poets are dead
And are only immortalized by books gathering dust?
I met one walking down a beaten path yesterday.
His every stride was rhythmic.
His stare was as moving as a sonnet.
When he opened his mouth,
A soliloquy tugged at my heartstrings,
A dam began,
A cistern burst forth with metaphors of hope;
Hope that springs from every word,
Every line and every tenet.
He spoke of the ordinary and the complexities of life,
Then he painted new and lost worlds with euphemisms and compelling similes.
His paint saturated every canvas of my mind,
Bringing him into the crevasses of my soul not previously canvased.
His stories chronicled the lives of those he'd met
Before me, those whose accounts were now told to me.
Though the grave holds many, poets still live.
I met one yesterday in my mind.

I met one who cried of being trapped in a time where
The fool's noise stifles the poet's pen;
The poet's art is traded for the joker's taunt,
Or for the novice's fifteen minutes of doom.
I met a poet who asked me
To delve deeper into the fountain of truth,
Where time stands still,
And words become personified.

I met a poet who compelled me
To hope and admonished me to the truth.
I met a poet who wasn't tangled by society's net,
Whose weapon is a two-edged sword
That wields power to cut the bone and marrow of your soul.
I met a poet whose truth went more in-depth
Than what words could speak,
Whose pen sometimes defy him when he slumbers
And writes for or against him.
His last words were, "Wake up, you sleeping poet.
The world needs you."
I woke up from my waking sleep to a canvas with infinite lines holding a pen
Whose ink begged to be the violent crucible of courage.

The Fool and His Heart

Away, tucked in a cellar, was his heart.
He had so recklessly given it to me,
And I, who had no use for it,
Tucked it away with my other undesirables.
He begged for my heart in exchange for his,
But I had no heart to give.
Oh, it was winter all year round,
And emptiness and sorrow covered under
The best smile and lie
I didn't want his heart,
And I tried to return it,
But he wouldn't take it back!
He tried to keep the water
From a cracked cistern to himself.
He begged me every day
To show him my heart,
But a blizzard had come,
And it never left.
It covered my heart beyond sight.
The squall was a fate brought on by a lover
Who used me as a pawn.
I, too, had left my soul in the back pocket of a fool.

Sunday Circus

Come Sunday morning, you take off your mask of sin and trade it for piety; because even though you sinned last night and even at breakfast, you made it to church. Round of applause for your blatant conceit! You strolled in like you somehow deserve a crown because, while others stayed home, you made it to church with your ten-piece to hand over to a thief. Oh no, not the one on the other side of Jesus, but a charlatan, a predator out to fleece. Can we have a moment of silence for the sheep who is so intent on the movement of the lion, it forgot to watch the hyena at its back?

Tell me, where did you get that awful sense of pride that you are better than others because you go to the Sunday circus every week? There are performers in God's house with guile on their lips, blame on their fingers, and resentment in their hearts, but like the Pharisees, they point fingers covered in their own shit. They are taking part in a Sunday circus while criticizing the rest of the world that wants no part of the charade.

You have a form of godliness that can't seem to reach beyond the confines of the four walls. When the young sisters come in from the cold, you turn up your noses at their clothes, the way they wear their hair, and the toll that life has so profoundly etched on their faces.

The church has become the bandage for your self-righteousness, for your holier-than-thou attitude and beliefs. You are in church, the place where you get a temporary salve for a festering sore that not even the pastor's best prayer and a thousand laying of hands can heal.

You are in the church, not out of love but out of burden and a sense of dreaded obligation when God calls you to freedom!

You are in church staging your having-it-all-together lies, holding on to malice in your hearts and silent hate over bruised egos and failure to stick with the Sunday script, but there you are.

You are in church, but no one outside wants to come in because they do not like the God you wear on your sleeves. You are called to be God's hands and feet extended, but he doesn't consider your acts pure because they are done to be seen by men. You promised God yes but have told those he sent no because they don't follow your Sunday script. They are not monkeying in your circus.
They are not a part of the religious elite. So, you build walls to separate you from them while barricading yourselves from the rest of humanity.

So now you own God? Does he belong to you and not us? Ode to the simple carpenter who doesn't parade his religious rhetoric, who is moved by the feelings of the commoner's infirmities and not his money. You are sugar-coating your demons to inflate your egos while people are out here dying from lost hope, looking for a savior in you. Still, you are unmoved by the infirmities of others because it's not your problem.

Stop bending over backward for high flaunting titles to affix to your repertoire of worldly accomplishments when we should be asking God for people and nations to impact.

He asked you to go out speaking the good news, but you, by and through your actions, teach others to hate your God because you live a life of bad news. You have forgotten the mercy extended to you when you were dirty rags made clean by a forgiving God. Others might sin differently than you, but are you within any right to point fingers? Are you? Someone is always watching. If our lives were like Bibles, the world would put them down because our talk and fruits oppose each other.

It's Sunday, and when the benediction is read, your mask of righteousness will be left in the pews. You will go on to live out the rest of the week with pride, overindulgence, pretenses, and failure to spread the good news. Everyone outside these four walls knows you have a form of godliness whose wick goes out as soon as you leave the church. No one at work wants your God because you are the cause of every discord, the slick devil, the chatty patty, the mean-face Angie, the too-holy-to-mingle Debra. Every Sunday, you are good news but terrible news during the week praising a God who can't smell his essence on you because you have missed him following a Sunday circus filled with characters playing parts in a plot the creator didn't write.

You have hidden what is most rotten in your temples behind vain words, righteous candor, and blatant hypocrisy. Now the cracks are breaking out of your masks like a volcano erupting with the very lava of your callousness and the decaying state of your hearts.

Still, you hold on, and as time passes, the world believes less in you because you shout God but have become distant strangers with him. Show the world something it can feel like a shoulder to cry on, hands that hold, ears that can be trusted, lips that whisper hope in the dying world.

Let your masks fall to the ground! The Sunday announcement is as follows: next Sunday, no shows are allowed!

Sister

Sister, you hold the universe in your soul and the world in your hand.
Your words quicken my spirit
And pull at my heartstrings.
Your stares compel me to freedom,
To love and to action.
So much has been thrown at you,
But you managed to pull
Your way through the muck.

Sister, I see you trying to keep your head above water
And marching to your own drum.
I have seen you used everything sent to take you off course and created a mosaic;
And when they asked you how you do it,
You told them you go with God.
Sister, can you introduce me to this "god" you speak of?

Sister, tell me why you walk with the gentleness of a dove
But have the fierceness of a lion?
Tell me why your hand and heart are open to even the least of men?

Tell me how the nightingales sing to you,
Why the sun kisses your skin,
Why the streams flow toward you,
And why the earth gives you of her bounty?

Sister, I beg you to tell me why you have pearls in your hair,
Prayers in your crown, and the kiss of heaven on your face?
Tell me of the glow you emanate, the effervescence of your spirit?
Sister, I see that charm doesn't deceive you,

That vanity is not your friend, and lust evades you.
Tell me, you who are fairer than rubies,
How you shine brightly in a world looking to snuff out your light?

Sister, I dream of walking with your grace, facing
Challenges with your strength, living with open arms,
Making wisdom the ornaments which keep my crown together, to love with the beauty of a dove,
To be as cunning as a fox and to bring each soul I meet to the light.

Sister, I know you don't need one more crown, but if I had one, I would lay it at your feet.

Song

I have a song whose tune comes alive
When I am on my bed,
A song that comforts my soul and is my refuge.
I have a song to heal my wounded soul.

The music of my heart is love
Which hangs on the strings of hope.
The song of my heart is peace with my past.
The song of my heart knocks on the door of the morning
And brings forth glee.
The song of my heart is love,
Love for the least and the greatest among me.
The song of my heart is echoed for all to hear,
For all to feel.
The song of my heart is called change,
It unhinges me from every weight
Which besets me and separates me
From the birth chord of the world.
The song of my heart is courage,
It causes me to scale walls and grow hinds' feet.
I have a song that keeps me company on my lonely bed.

Oh, Woman Don't You Weep

Mama said, "Don't you weep,
Baby, don't you mourn."
Papa said, "Daughter,
You got to put your shoulders to the wheel."
My one true friend said,
"Be like the pig. Wash in the first water you see."
But my soul was anchored by a thousand bricks,
My heart filled with disappointment and guile.

Mama said, "Baby, you better save your tears.
You goin' need them someday."
Papa said, "Child pull up your bootstraps.
It's about to be a long walk."
My one true friend told me,
"Friend, your low place is your high place."
But my soul was held down by the weight of two oceans
And the sting of regret.

Oh, my heart was a fountain of sorrow,
And my tears were my pillow, my food.
My bed was soaked in the river of my tears,
For I had given looters free passage to my treasury,
And I had given dogs what was holy.

Then I heard God say, "It is time to rejoice.
Take up your bed and walk."
The light then returned, and laughter burst forth like a cistern from my soul.
I wept no more.

Insta-Lie

Mirror, mirror on the wall,
Could you hide my broken pieces, these flaws?
Tap two times to let me know—
I am beautiful—
I've put on this makeup, not for me but for you.
Oh, I need to get my fix—
A fix of likes and comments
From strangers who don't know I have an ugly inside
Filled with dead man's bones, pain, hurt, regrets.

Oh, I need to get my fix, one last hit
Cause I am a fiend — a fiend
For validation and pacification.
Don't you know what lies behind
The make-belief, the insta-lie?
But who cares?
Cause I am insta-fine, insta-fly
Living in my insta-lies,
Buried in debt to live a fallacy.
Oh, silly me!

Mirror, mirror on the wall,
Can you hide my bad news,
While I perfume this dirty laundry, this stink, no one smells but me?
ROL. Is that an Insta-date for an instant-like? Ha-ha!

Mirror, mirror, I am itching for a hit.
Can you hide my scars behind filters,
As I write shallow captions and parrot the lives of people I barely even know?

Mirror, mirror on the wall,
Tell me I am pretty.
Come on! Look at me!
Cause my world is upside down
And I am losing it! I'm losing my shit.
I need a fix, a hit, a score.
Mirror, tell me something good, please?
So I can mask the pain and the lies—
This disease called fantasy.
Oh, silly me!
Mirror, mirror, are you there?
Are you there?

I Am Queen

I was washed in the waters of En Gedi—
And colored by the sun.
I am anointed with the oil of my creator's olive vineyard.
I am Jewel of the Nile,
A burgeoning oasis,
Giver of life, mother of humanity.
I am queen.

I am a child of the sun,
Daughter of the universe!
I was nested in the garden of Eden.
And planted like a cypress tree in the Sahara.
I traversed the waters of the Americas from the Gold Coast,
I am queen,
Bold, beautiful, brave!
I am queen,
Bold, beautiful, brave.
Each time you see me,
I bare my soul before you,
My frailties, obstacles, and voice of reason.

I am a sojourner in a foreign land,
A byword, at times an eyesore.
I have taken on strange customs, tongues, and mores,
While disregarding mine,
Yet, I am hardly seen as an equal.
My heroism is often met with indifference and scorn
Because I was taught to be everything but myself.
My silence is welcomed, but no, my voice is muzzled by false narratives and conjectures.

I wear my hair in an afro, in Bantu knots, in braids
To remind you of my defiance to your status quo.
I will no longer conform to ideals that diminish who I am
Or beg for a seat at tables I am not invited to.
I will walk with the stride of the queens before me
And sashay down the halls of repression in my heels.
I take off any robe soaked with society's facades
Because it is drenched with the weight of my tears.
My tears are an ever-flowing stream
Of the issues of my life and my oppression.

What lies behind my makeup are the tell-tale signs
Of my pain, my burdens.
My dress covers the scars on my back,
My wounds, my secret scarlet.
I am hogtied to imposed limitations,
But today, I break free because
I am queen!

Oh, come, let me unveil so that you can see my scars.
I now stand before you bare,
Stripped, naked.
Come, let me show you, my humanity.
I have been dispossessed of everything,
But my resolve and my fight
I have been beaten and stretched
By indifference, verbal, and physical conflicts.
Yet, I maneuver with
Acceptance, grace, and forgiveness;
I have been looted, raped, beaten, denied, and judged.

Can you not see it? Can you not hear it?
That I am the pulse of my ancestors,
Their echo, their pain, their deferred hope.

I am a queen,
Bold, beautiful, human.
I am a queen,
Bold, beautiful, human.
I am a queen,
Bold, beautiful, human.

When you see me,
I hope you see my humanity
As I see yours.
I am the ebb and the flow of the light within me.
I am the precise manifestation of God.
Can you see me — now, now, now!
Oh, I am queen.

The Culling

The sheepherder returned to find his flock culled.
He had gone in search of a lost sheep,
But when he came back,
Jackals and foxes gleaned the fold.

With his lost sheep on his bosom,
The shepherd went looking for his other sheep.
Word had spread to the other drovers
That there was a thinning of the herd— everywhere.

Truth is naked, but lies wear a crown
And stand in a lofty place.
Everyone wants to be king
While they grab figs to cover their nakedness.

The sheepherder risked his life
For a fold that did not want to stay grounded.
It followed the cry of the foxes,
Lock, stock, and barrel.

The shepherd boy had sounded the harp—
To get the lamb, the ewe, and the ram
To the mountaintop,
But the silly sheep followed the pigs into the sea.
The shepherd wept for his dying flock.

You have come to the end of the poetic journey.

CONNECT WITH TRISHFORREAL

WWW.TRISHFORREAL.COM

www.ingramcontent.com/pod-product-compliance
Lightning Source LLC
Chambersburg PA
CBHW072004290426
44109CB00018B/2125